Compliments of the Chef

Great Recipes from the Innovative Restaurants and Cafés of Berkeley and the East Bay

Revised and Expanded Edition

Ruth Dorman and Lois Marcus with Paul T. Johnston

Illustrated by Ruth Dorman
Foreword by Marion Cunningham
Preface to the new edition by Narsai David

Aris Books

Addison-Wesley Publishing Company, Inc.
Reading, Massachusetts   Menlo Park, California   New York
Don Mills, Ontario   Wokingham, England   Amsterdam   Bonn
Sydney   Singapore   Tokyo   Madrid   San Juan

Many of the designations used by manufacturers and sellers to distinguish their products are claimed as trademarks. Where those designations appear in this book and Addison-Wesley was aware of a trademark claim, the designations have been printed with initial capital letters (e.g., Grand Marnier liqueur).

"Bread Garden" is a registered trademark of the Bread Garden Bakery.

Library of Congress Cataloging-in-Publication Data

Compliments of the chef : great recipes from the innovative
   restaurants and cafes of Berkeley and the East Bay / Ruth Dorman and
   Lois Marcus with Paul T. Johnston : illustrated by Ruth Dorman. —
   Rev.
      p. cm.
   Includes index.
   ISBN 0-201-19626-3
    1. Cookery, International. 2. Cookery—California.
   3. Restaurants, lunch rooms, etc.—California. I. Dorman, Ruth.
   II. Marcus, Lois. III. Johnston, Paul T., 1950–
   TX725.A1C574 1989
   641.59—dc19   88-36492
                                                    CIP

Aris Books Editorial Offices and
Test Kitchen
1621 Fifth Street
Berkeley, CA 94710
(415) 527-5171

Project Editor: Carolyn Miller
Book Designer: Jeanne Jambu and Kajun Graphics
Cover Designer: Copenhaver Cumpston
Cover Photographer: Marshall Berman

Set in 10 point Berkeley Oldstyle by DEKR Corp., Woburn, MA

ABCDEFGHIJ-VB-89
First printing, April 1989

TABLE OF CONTENTS

FOREWORD BY MARION CUNNINGHAM iii

ACKNOWLEDGMENTS iv

PREFACE BY NARSAI DAVID vii

A CHEF'S INTRODUCTION 1

INGREDIENTS 6

BASICS 17

Techniques 17

Recipes 19

RESTAURANTS

À LA CARTE 23

AUGUSTA'S 25

BAY WOLF RESTAURANT 28

BETTE'S OCEANVIEW DINER 32

BETTE'S-TO-GO 35

BOMBAY CUISINE 38

BREAD GARDEN 41

BRITT-MARIE'S 44

BROADWAY TERRACE CAFÉ 48

CAFÉ FANNY 53

CAFÉ GLENDA 56

CAFÉ PASTORAL 59

CHEESE BOARD 63

CHEZ PANISSE 65

CHRISTOPHER'S CAFÉ 70

CLAREMONT HOTEL 75

COCOLAT 78

FATAPPLE'S 81

FOURTH STREET GRILL   84

GERTIE'S CHESAPEAKE BAY CAFÉ   87

GIOVANNI'S   89

GULF COAST OYSTER BAR   91

HUNAN PALACE   94

INN KENSINGTON   97

KATHLEEN'S DOYLE STREET CAFÉ   99

LA CRÈME DE LA CRÈME   102

LALIME'S   105

LIPPZ BISTRO   108

METROPOLE   111

MUDD'S   114

NADINE RESTAURANT   117

NAKAPAN   120

NAN YANG RESTAURANT   123

NORMAN'S   126

OLIVETO CAFÉ AND RESTAURANT   129

OMNIVORE   132

PANINI   137

PASTA SHOP   141

PICANTE TAQUERÍA & CANTINA   143

POULET   146

RIERA'S   149

RISTORANTE VENEZIA AND CAFFE VENEZIA   153

SANTA FE BAR & GRILL   156

SEDONA GRILL & BAR   159

SIAM CUISINE   163

SPENGER'S FISH GROTTO   166

THORNHILL CAFÉ   168

TOURELLE CAFÉ AND RESTAURANT   170

VASILIO'S KITCHEN   173

WALKER'S PIE SHOP   176

YENCHING   178

ZACHARY'S CHICAGO PIZZA   181

RESTAURANT INDEX   185

RECIPE INDEX   189

GENERAL INDEX   195

FOREWORD

*I*f cooking and eating are important to you, then this book is a vital guide to our new culinary direction. The same energy and vitality that was spent during the rebellious sixties on campuses all over the country, and especially on the University of California campus in Berkeley, is now being spent in many Berkeley and East Bay area restaurants producing wonderful food. The philosophy of this new cooking idiom is one of rebellion against the vast anonymous world in which we live, with its processed foods touched only by machine, its crops harvested by machine, its loss of quality, and most of all, its loss of individual significance.

The new cooks have restored a sense of personal importance to the culinary scene by being completely in charge of food preparation. The typical Berkeley restaurant is small, which allows better control. The old culinary rules and traditions have been put aside, and the chef searches for the purest and best ingredients to combine in innovative ways. The result of all this is a new group of sparkling restaurants that are, in no insignificant way, influencing American eating and dining habits.

Here then is a collection of excellent recipes offered by the chefs of many of the area's finest restaurants. Chef Paul T. Johnston's introduction is intelligent and interesting, and he has done an admirable job of scaling down the recipes so they can be easily reproduced at home. And bravo! to the authors and the Sisterhood of Congregation Beth El—you've proven once again that dedication and service can produce work of great value.

Marion Cunningham

PREFACE TO THE REVISED EDITION

In the sixties at the Potluck Restaurant we felt we were competing with San Francisco as there were so few fine restaurants in the East Bay. By the seventies, the creative energies of the new generation started focusing on food and wine and a restaurant revolution was underway! Although we call it *new*, it was in fact a return to the basics. The freshest foods, very simply grilled and garnished with bouquets of herbs, were the mainstay. We discovered the elegant simplicity of red or yellow peppers, puréed to make a sauce. Goat cheese started fermenting right here in northern California and, along with extra-virgin olive oil, became a buzz word for food writers.

The whole country now looks to Berkeley and neighboring areas for inspiration, and the ultimate compliment to our chefs is that America's freshest cooking is often referred to as California Cuisine.

These recipes are a collection from the East Bay's most creative chefs and finest restaurants. Each one has been tested for use in a home kitchen and should immediately recall many memorable dinners in those restaurants.

Narsai David

Rack of Lamb Assyrian

Although Narsai no longer operates a restaurant in Berkeley, we felt that no cookbook about dining in the East Bay would be complete without including some of his recipes. So here are two of Narsai's hallmarks, Rack of Lamb Assyrian and Chocolate Decadence.

Marinade

This is one of the recipes that made Narsai's a popular restaurant in the seventies and early to mid-eighties.

1 large onion
2 or 3 cloves garlic
1 teaspoon dried basil leaves
½ cup pomegranate juice (or less of concentrate)
¼ cup dry red wine
½ teaspoon salt
½ teaspoon pepper

2½ lamb racks, each with 8 or 9 ribs (see Note)

In a blender or food processor purée the marinade ingredients. Rub the marinade well into the racks. Place the racks in a shallow glass or enameled pan and pour the remaining marinade over them. Marinate in the refrigerator overnight or at a cool room temperature for 6 to 8 hours.

If it has been kept in the refrigerator, let the meat come to room temperature—which will take about 45 minutes—before roasting. Preheat the oven to 450°.

When ready to cook, wipe off any excess marinade and roast the racks for 15 to 20 minutes for medium rare, longer if you like lamb done to a greater degree. *Serves 6.*

NOTE: Ask the butcher to remove the chine bone and the lifter meat and to French-cut the rib bones.

Chocolate Decadence

This cake needs to be frozen before serving, so allow the time.

Cake

1 pound semisweet chocolate, broken into
    squares
10 tablespoons (1¼ sticks) unsalted butter
4 whole eggs
1 tablespoon sugar
1 tablespoon flour

Topping

1½ cups heavy cream
1 teaspoon vanilla extract
1 tablespoon sugar
Shaved chocolate
1 package (10–12 ounces) frozen raspberries,
    defrosted

Flour and butter an 8-inch cake pan and line it with paper. Preheat the oven to 425°.

Put the chocolate and butter in the top of a double boiler and heat until the chocolate is just melted. Set aside.

In the top of another double boiler, beat the eggs and sugar until the sugar dissolves and the mixture is lukewarm (do not overcook). Remove from the heat and whip until the mixture thickens and is about quadrupled in volume. Fold the flour into the thickened egg mixture. Stir a quarter of the flour and egg mixture into the melted chocolate, then fold the chocolate back into the remaining egg mixture.

Pour the batter into the prepared cake pan and shake gently to level it. Bake for 15 minutes (the cake will still be runny in the center). Cool briefly, then freeze, preferably overnight, before removing the cake from the pan.

To unmold, carefully dip the bottom of the pan into hot water to loosen the cake. When it will move easily, unmold it onto a cake plate. Peel off the paper and discard.

Whip the heavy cream, adding the vanilla and sugar as it thickens. Mask the cake with the whipped cream and decorate the top with shaved chocolate. Refrigerate until ready to serve.

Shortly before serving, purée the defrosted raspberries in a blender and press through a fine sieve to remove the seeds. Spoon the raspberry purée around the cake or spoon some of the purée around individual slices. *Serves 12.*

ACKNOWLEDGMENTS

Sisterhoods and cookbooks seem to go together like . . . Berkeley and great restaurants. It was a combination we couldn't resist when we compiled the first edition. And we couldn't resist revising and updating the book, now with one hundred seventy-five exceptional recipes from many of the area's most distinctive, and some of the newest, restaurants, bakeries, cafés, and delis.

We are indebted to the owners and chefs of these establishments, who graciously responded to our requests and parted with their cherished recipes.

I don't think any of us in the Sisterhood anticipated the amount of work that would ensue when one of our members, Matilde Hollander, rekindled our interest in producing a cookbook. Each Sisterhood member involved has generously and enthusiastically given hours and hours of time to this project. Our sincere thanks go to Donna Weinberg, Ruth Dorman, and Roz Plishner, who not only solicited recipes but also shopped for and participated in the lengthy recipe-testing process in Aris's test kitchen.

The considerable talents of our illustrator, Ruth Dorman, are showcased throughout this book, and her contributions to every aspect of its production cannot be overstated. Lois

Schwartz undertook the enormous task of word processing and editing the manuscript and was also an invaluable contributor to the restaurant write-ups. We also benefited from the legal counsel of Judy Koster and from the writing and editing skills of many others.

For this revised edition, we followed the same formula that worked so well originally: We collected recipes from the area's new restaurants, cafés, bakeries, and delis, and tested them with Chef Paul Johnston at the Aris Test Kitchen. Along with the updated material from the first edition, and with a fond farewell to those noble establishments that for a variety of reasons are no longer with us, we believe that this new edition admirably represents the still-evolving culinary creativity of Berkeley and the East Bay.

And finally, again, our sincere thanks to Aris Books. We are indebted to John Harris and the Aris/Addison-Wesley staff for gently guiding us, with patience and good humor, through the ins and outs of professional cookbook publishing.

Lois Marcus
Sisterhood of Congregation Beth El
Berkeley, California

A CHEF'S INTRODUCTION

This book comes directly from the professional kitchens of Berkeley and the East Bay, through the diligence of the volunteers of the Sisterhood of Congregation Beth El. As a chef and former (and probably future) restaurant owner, I speak the restaurant language and am the translator for this book, formulating recipes for the home kitchen using material from the very different environment of the restaurant kitchen. The greatest challenge has been to do this in all consciousness of, and with all respect for, the spirit of the recipe and the dish it represents. My goal, and that of Aris Books, has been to give you a recipe that, when followed precisely, will give an honest approximation of the actual dish, for a recipe can never be exact.

And it has been an amusing task as well, knowing the time constraints that force a chef to scribble a recipe on the back of his shopping list while the volunteer from the Sisterhood waits, lucky that even though he had forgotten the appointment, she has managed to catch him and he has the presence of mind to jot the recipe down. So we often got shorthand versions of recipes, often had to go back to the chef with questions, and often had to rely on my intuition.

It has been an education to approach the work of my colleagues in this way. I am more accustomed to eating their work, being inspired by it, or talking about it than I am to trying to replicate it in a domestic kitchen. I have learned some new techniques, particularly in the fields of Chinese and Southeast Asian cooking and, not being a baker by predilection, have picked up a few things about bread and desserts that are sure to come in handy some day.

It is important, in trying to understand these recipes, to take their original environment into consideration. The resources, equipment, and manpower available to a chef in his own restaurant are quite unlike anything to be found at home. The chef has a staff that can provide everything from peeled garlic and onions to basic stocks and sauces, as well as such specialized ingredients as any amount of a certain vegetable cut to specific dimensions. A chef has many functions, which vary with the restaurant, and may include planning menus and developing new recipes; food cost and buying (including trips to markets); hiring, firing, and training cooks, and sometimes dishwashers; and actual food production during and before service. And often, the chef owns the restaurant!

With so much responsibility, a chef needs as many resources as possible, the most important of which is input from coworkers. When a kitchen is really alive, the ideas come from everyone, and no chef can claim complete authorship of a recipe. Somewhere, in the background at least, is the suggestion of some other cook, or maybe even the dishwasher, who pointed out that a certain dish was coming back from the table only half eaten.

Where Do Recipes Come From?

Where does a recipe come from, and how does it work in the restaurant? Let's take a look at the kitchen first. A restaurant kitchen, depending on the size of the establishment, usually breaks down into three stations: pasta and sauté, grill or broiler, and salad (also called pantry). If the restaurant is large or the culinary emphasis is away from the grill, pasta and sauté become two separate stations. If the restaurant is small, the grill and sauté stations may merge, and the pantry and pasta may be handled by the same person. But as an example, let's take a grill-oriented restaurant of about seventy-five seats, requiring the three basic stations, sauté, grill, and pantry. A waiter hands in an order for a table of four. It reads:

Table: 7   No. of guests: 4   Waiter: Joe
1 Caesar Salad
2 Timbales
1 Tomato Basil Fettuccine
1 Salmon (Grilled)
1 Chicken Paillard
1 Salmon (Sautéed)
1 Chicken Goat Cheese Linguine

In this kitchen, the pasta and sauté station is first in line, so it gets the orders and coordinates timing (also called expediting). The cook looks at the ticket and sees that the appetizers are all cold and all come from the salad station. She relays the order to the pantry. The pantry cook unmolds and dresses the timbales, which will not suffer while he makes the Caesar salad. He breaks coddled eggs into the bowl he keeps for the Caesars, whisks in the dressing to emulsify, tosses in a handful of prepared romaine lettuce, sprinkles in anchovies, grated Parmesan cheese, and croutons, tosses the salad with his hands, arranges it on the plate, and sets it on the counter. "Up on seven," he calls to the sauté cook. She rings the waiter. He arrives immediately, knowing that a Caesar salad wilts within minutes, and serves his table their first course.

A few minutes later, the waiter says "Fire pasta on seven, please." The sauté cook ignites a burner and in a sauté pan pours olive oil from a wine bottle. In go pine nuts to toast for a minute, then a spoonful of garlic purée for a second, then a splash of white wine and a handful of roasted tomatoes with the flame left high. She flicks up the burner control for the pasta water, which, kept at a simmer already, is engulfed by flame and instantly comes to a rolling boil. She throws in a handful of fresh pasta, gives the sauté pan with the sauce a shake, and adds salt and a pinch of fresh-ground pepper. The sauce is reduced to her satisfaction and she removes it from the fire, adds fresh-chopped basil, tastes the sauce, lifts the basket out of the pasta pan, shakes the noodles dry, adds them to the sauce, tosses the whole works in the air a couple of times to mix it, and slides it on the plate. One hand sprinkles grated Parmesan cheese over the pasta, while the other adds a strewing of chopped parsley. The plate goes up on the counter, and the sauté cook rings the waiter.

As the waiter picks up the pasta, the sauté cook turns to the grill cook and says "Fire four," because she knows that by the time the kitchen has finished cooking the entrées, those four people will have finished their pasta. Nonetheless, the waiter shows up a minute later and repeats the "fire" order. This kind of double-checking has saved his life many times and the kitchen always appreciates it. (Bear in mind that a seventy-five-seat dining room has fifteen to twenty-five tables and the kitchen can be looking at as many as fifteen to twenty tickets at once.) The sauté cook has already prepared the sauce for the pasta (she did it at the same time as the tomato-basil pasta), and she now flours the piece of salmon and starts it cooking in a small sauté pan. The grill cook puts his piece of salmon on and, after waiting a minute, puts the chicken paillard on the grill, having given the thick salmon fillet a head start. He glances at the sauté station to gauge his coworker's progress on table No. 7 (as well as several other tables in progress). He pulls out two plates and arranges the garnishes, turns to two other tables that were just fired, and flips the salmon and the paillard.

Meanwhile, the sauté cook throws another order of pasta in the water, removes the salmon to a warm plate, and splashes brandy into the sauté pan. Flames billow, then die, and she adds a spoonful of cream sauce base complete with mushrooms, pours in a splash of cream, stirs rapidly with a whisk, adds a shake of salt and a few drops of lemon juice from a wine bottle, tastes, and pours the sauce over the salmon. The grill cook lifts the salmon and chicken from the grill together, puts them on their plates, spoons a dollop of basil butter on the salmon and one of ancho chili butter on the chicken, then slides over and finishes the salmon plate for the sauté cook while she drains the pasta and tosses it with the sauce. It has thickened a bit, so she adds a splash of chicken stock, heats the whole for a second, slides it on the plate, arranges a fan of red pepper julienne over the top, inserts a sprig of mint as garnish, and rings the waiter.

Scenes like this occur every night in hundreds of permutations all over Berkeley, indeed, all over the world. This is the world of the professional cook, where preparedness for the rush is of paramount importance and as few words as possible are spoken between workers to accomplish the end of artfully feeding as many people as the restaurant will hold.

With this sample of restaurant life in mind, it is easy to see the difficulty of formulating a recipe at all, much less one that works dependably at home. Most restaurant recipes are never written down, but are transmitted orally and by demonstration, or are reinvented at every execution, changing to accommodate ingredients and moods.

Where Do Chefs Come From?

In addition to the physical setting there is a host of other influences affecting the cuisine from which these recipes arise. The Bay Area is a vast melting pot of peoples, their cooking, and their ingredients, and this affects anyone who cooks here. Berkeley and its environs have been the site of a unique confluence of politics with education in fields such as nutrition and literature, which, combined with a stagnation of the economy, left college-educated people with more job opportunities in food service than in their chosen field.

A hypothetical, though not necessarily typical example of the making of a chef might be that of a brand-new Ph.D. in history with no money and no job. Unable to leave town, our disgruntled graduate gets a job prepping in a restaurant, and soon realizes that in addition to his European travel experience, his intelligence, and his basic arts training he has a special and exciting sensitivity to food. The restaurant not being one of the best, and the habit of political rebellion still strong, we have here a culinary revolutionary, a person who remembers amazing meals in France, Spain, Italy, and Mexico and sets out to reinterpret them. Skills learned in a professional but uninspired restaurant setting soon lend ability to the tremendous drive of an open mind and exploring curiosity.

There are many versions of this story, many men and women who found that what they thought was their career training was really just a way of getting ready to cook, and—with the Chez Panisse group foremost and earliest—these chefs have taken the variety of cuisines and ingredients in the Bay Area and, with openness, honesty, and imagination, have woven a style no longer in revolt against older cooking modes but a logical extension of them, a cuisine with classical underpinnings and a wholly American character.

What Is California Cuisine?

Although the cuisine that has emerged is hard to define (some practitioners even objecting to the inescapable, but misleading appellation of "California cuisine"), it does have some clear outlines. This style of cooking relies heavily on ingredients of the highest quality and freshness. The emphasis is on simplicity, with extensive use of the mesquite grill and a general direction strongly away from the heaviness associated with French haute cuisine, although many French techniques are of central importance. Sauces are thickened with purées of fruit or vegetables; or by reductions of rich stocks; or by butter worked into, and emulsified by, a strongly acid reduction of citrus juices, wine, vinegar, or fruit juices, or a mixture of these elements. (The basic sauce of this family is called *beurre blanc* and is drawn directly from French cuisine. It is discussed at length in the Basics section). Other characteristics include vegetables cooked *al dente* at most, an emphasis on seafood and away from beef (perhaps in revolt against the steakhouse cooking we all grew up on), and a "smaller is better" attitude resulting in an affection for baby vegetables and lettuces, as well as very young chickens and lamb. In fact, there is a near-fetish regarding ingredients in the Berkeley area, with sources zealously sought and jealously protected and prices inexorably reflecting demand.

One of the most distinctive features of the recent culinary revolution in and around Berkeley is a bold amalgamation of cuisines, with exotic ingredients and techniques made to speak a new language, and elements of non-European cookery finding their way into the most unorthodox settings. Among the influential non-European cuisines in the area are Chinese, Southeast Asian, Mexican and Southwest American, Japanese, and traditional American home and country cookery. While Los Angeles has its Franco-Japanese trend, we have Fourth Street Grill serving two weeks of Indonesian foods; Christopher's Café mixing Chinese, Southeast Asian, French, and California mesquite grill cookery; and frequent appearances of Indian food at Omnivore. Chefs can be found using lemon grass in marinades of their own formulation. Papaya may find its way into a composed butter or a salad dressing, and other "exotic" elements such as an array of Indian spices, dried Persian limes, dried chilies, Italian dried tomatoes, assorted caviars, and *galangal*, may turn up in heretofore unfamiliar circumstances and combinations. (These and other unusual items are discussed in more detail in the Ingredients section.)

Along with the "new California" restaurants found in this book are other restaurants that are either wholly ethnic or deserve institutional status for having survived decades in the toughest business Dun and Bradstreet ever rated.

The Berkeley/East Bay food phenomenon is the result of experimentation and unbridled creativity. Working on the revised edition of *Compliments*, which allowed me to visit and work with old friends, has convinced me that the creativity is still alive and expanding. I hope the reader will enjoy discovering the new recipes and restaurants represented in this edition, as well as rediscovering old favorites.

Paul T. Johnston

INGREDIENTS

It is basic to the Berkeley culinary phenomenon that all ingredients are special and that the ingredients dictate the recipe, not the other way around. Many of the area's best dishes are the result of conforming the cooking to the best ingredients available. While the purpose of this section is to describe some of the unusual ingredients used in this book, it should be remembered that one aim of this kind of cooking is not necessarily to use a certain unusual thing, but to use the *best* ingredients, unusual or not.   PTJ

Bamboo Shoots

The presliced bamboo shoots available in supermarkets are tasteless and have poor texture. Canned whole bamboo shoots are a great improvement. Before using them, slice them in half lengthwise and rinse them well under running water and slice to the desired size. *Sources*: Some regular grocery stores may carry whole bamboo shoots, but the best bet is an Asian grocery store. Some Asian markets are now carrying fresh bamboo shoots packed in water.

Butter

Most of the recipes in this book were tested using unsalted butter; when we consider it especially important to a recipe, it is specified.

Salt is used in butter not so much as a flavoring as it is a preservative; saltiness often covers up a certain amount of rancidity. The objection to salted butter is not to the salt but to the possible lack of freshness. Sweet butter can be tricky to buy. Get it from a store with a high turnover. If you are not going to use it within a few days, freeze most of it, as it will go rancid. If you have doubts about the butter you are going to buy, unwrap a corner and smell it. If there is the slightest hint of sourness, go elsewhere. *Sources*: Most supermarkets and grocery stores.

Chicken Breasts

Boneless chicken breasts are used extensively in this book. You can either bone them yourself or have the butcher do it. (An old-fashioned poultry shop is ideal for this.) When buying chicken breasts to bone, avoid the halved breasts sold in most grocery stores. They are hard to work with. Also, since they are rarely split in half accurately, there is usually a lot of waste.

Chilies and Peppers

Used in Mexican, Asian, Mediterranean, and California cooking, the chili in its hundreds of varieties is used sometimes as a vegetable, sometimes as a seasoning.

Bell Peppers

The familiar green bell pepper turns red when ripe, becoming sweeter and more complex-tasting in the process. Other varieties turn golden yellow or even black. They are eaten raw in salads, are used roasted and peeled in many different preparations, and are eaten as a vegetable. *Sources:* Widely available in supermarkets and grocery stores.

Fresh Chilies

Fresh chilies figure largely in local cooking, as an object of a heat fetish and as the source of unique flavors. The heat of chili in some dishes is not just a physical sensation, but an integral part of the flavor structure. There are hundreds of different chilies. Following are the ones used in this book, listed in order of diminishing heat. Be advised, however, that the heat of fresh chilies varies; one batch of *jalapeños* may be bland, while the supposedly mild Fresno chili can sometimes knock your socks off.

Thai Chili: This is the hottest commercially grown chili we have ever met; it has driven seasoned jalapeño eaters to gasping despair. It is a tiny chili, ¼ inch wide and 2 to 3 inches long, but watch out. Like all peppers, it turns red when ripe.

Jalapeño Chili: This is a widely available chili. It is dark green, often with bluish-black shadings, about an inch wide and 2- to 3-inches long, with a blunt, rounded shape. When cut open, it has a pungent aroma that is an indication of its heat. The stronger the aroma, the hotter the chili. This is the chili to use in most Thai dishes, unless the Thai chili is called for. When ripe, the jalapeño turns red, has a sweeter flavor and is at its absolute hottest.

Serrano Chili: A small chili that packs a mighty wallop. Some consider it hotter than the jalapeño About 2 inches long and ½ inch wide, it is a lighter green than the jalapeño and some turn yellow and red when ripe. The *serrano* has a taste reminiscent of black pepper and is much used in *salsa crudas.*

Fresno Chili: This is a milder chili, sometimes with only a hint of heat. It is similar in size to a jalapeño but conical in shape and a lighter green. When ripe, they turn beautiful yellows and reds. They are good to use when the flavor of chili is wanted but not the heat.

Pasilla, Poblano, and Anaheim Chilies: These are usually but *not* always mild chilies. The Anaheim is about 6 inches long and 1½ inches wide, and pale green in color. The *poblano* and *pasilla* are both dark green and roughly 3-inch elongated triangles. These chilies turn red when ripe and are dried at that stage, when they are often mildly hot. They have tough skins when fresh and should be peeled. *Sources:* Fresh chilies are found in the greatest variety in produce markets serving

Latin or Asian populations. Some gourmet markets are beginning to carry fresh chilies.

Dried Chilies

Dried chilies are important flavorings in Mexican cooking and are available in vast variety. Although not much used in this book, they do play a significant part in the cooking of some Berkeley chefs. The most widely used dried chilies, outside of Mexican cuisine, are the hottest ones, from cayenne to red pepper flakes. Cayenne is made from a small African red chili. Red pepper flakes are usually made from the Japanese red chili. It is often best to make your own pepper flakes, because the flavor begins to dissipate on grinding, leaving nothing but heat. The other commonly used dried chilies are made from larger ripe chilies such as the *ancho, poblano,* and *pasilla.* They are usually mildly hot, being used for their flavor, not their heat. *Sources:* Dried chilies can be found in Mexican markets.

Clarified Butter

Perhaps the finest of cooking oils, clarified butter is butter with the moisture and milk solids removed. It tolerates very high heat and lends the flavor and body of butter to a dish. It is expensive, about double the price of butter, and it requires a little effort to make. There are several methods for making it. The simplest (but not the best) is to melt butter and then chill it. The butterfat will rise to the top, and the liquid and solids will sink to the bottom. The problem is separating the two components without wasting butter or getting unwanted moisture in the clarified butter. A better, but more time-consuming method is to gently simmer melted butter. The milk solids will appear at the top as foam, where they can be skimmed off. The moisture will simply evaporate. There are more elaborate methods, for which you might consult an Indian cookbook recipe, for ghee.

Coconut Milk

Most restaurants use canned coconut milk, and we have found that the frozen varieties are best. Siam Cuisine specifies a Thai brand. All of these are basically a purée of fresh coconut meat. Sweetened coconut milk is for desserts and piña coladas and does not work for these recipes. You can make your own coconut milk by soaking finely grated fresh or dried coconut in hot water for about an hour, then puréeing the mixture in a blender and straining out the liquid. Generally two or three extractions are made from the same meat, and many recipes specify different uses for each extraction. For these recipes, make two extractions and combine them. Homemade coconut milk will be a different strength than the canned (probably weaker, having a greater water content) so pay close attention to the liquid level of your dish and cook it down if necessary. *Sources*: Thai, Vietnamese, Indian, and Chinese grocery stores; some gourmet markets or delis; the frozen-food case of large grocery stores.

Crème Fraîche

Crème fraîche is simply cultured heavy cream. It is widely used as a substitute for heavy cream and sour cream. Since it is cultured, it has a slightly sour, cheesy taste. Unlike sour cream, it can be boiled without curdling. It can also be whipped and sweetened and used in desserts.

To make *crème fraîche*, add ¼ cup of buttermilk or unflavored yogurt to 2 cups of heavy cream. Mix well and let the mixture stand in a warm place overnight or until the desired sourness is achieved.

Dried Lemon Leaves

A component of Indonesian and Thai cooking, dried lemon leaves are just that and not really so exotic, especially if you have a lemon tree in your backyard. That's your ingredient right there, on the ground. Like lemon grass, lemon leaves have the taste of lemon without the acidity. *Sources*: Southeast Asian grocers or the backyard.

Dried Limes and Lime Leaves

Dried limes are available whole, called "dried Kaffir limes," or in the form of strips of dried peel. They have an intense lime flavor and an aroma made more complex by the drying process, and are used in Thai and Indonesian curries and some Mideastern dishes, as are the dried leaves. The limes are used crushed, the leaves are used whole or crumbled, the dried peel whole. Both the peel and the leaves are often called *makrud* or *macrut*. *Sources*: Asian or Mideastern grocery stores.

Fish Sauce

Fish sauce is one of those foreign seasonings we could call exotic but which a not-so-openminded person might call weird. It looks like soy sauce, but is lighter in color, and serves the same function, as a source of salt and flavor depth, but it actually consists of the brine from pickled fish. This gives it a distinctive aroma. Fish sauce is an essential ingredient of Southeast Asian cooking; it cannot be omitted without affecting the flavor of a dish. The fishy odor is noticeable only before cooking. The saltiness varies with the brand; you should taste first and adjust the recipe accordingly. In general, fish sauce is twice as salty as soy sauce. *Sources*: Thai, Vietnamese, or Chinese grocers.

Galangal

Related to ginger, *galangal* is a recent discovery to most of us in this country. It looks like ginger, but is woodier and has an aroma like genuine spirits of turpentine (which is not to be confused with paint thinner). Used mainly for seasoning soups and stews, it is hard to find in the fresh state, but is available in powdered form (called *laos* powder) and as dried slices. The dried slices are tough and woody and should be powdered in a blender or food processor, or simmered in the dish and removed before serving. *Sources*: Thai, Vietnamese, or Indian grocers; sometimes found fresh in produce markets.

Garlic

Garlic is nearly a cult food, and a lot of it is eaten in Berkeley. Vital to most cuisines and a source of both powerful and subtle flavors, its importance cannot be overstated. When shopping for garlic, look for large heads with large cloves. Small cloves are hard to peel and dry out quickly. As with other foods, freshness is important, and if you have never had garlic fresh out of the ground, it is worth the trouble. Fresh garlic is more delicate and fragrant than older garlic, which starts to become acrid after a few months. Look for garlic that is still moist between the cloves, with the dividing parchment soft and pliable rather than crisp and papery. Avoid using cloves that are yellowed and withered. Avoid those little cellophane-wrapped boxes traditionally sold in supermarkets. Look for a produce market where the bulbs are displayed openly in a bin. And if you don't like what is displayed, ask if they have anything fresher in the back. Produce markets buy most of their year's garlic in July and August when the American garlic crop is harvested. Mexican garlic is harvested twice a year, and can be superb. When you do find a good batch, buy a month's worth and store it in a cool, dark place away from moisture. *Sources*: Produce markets, ethnic grocery stores, gourmet markets.

Ginger

A pungent rhizome widely used in Asian cookery. The ginger used in this book is almost always fresh. *Sources*: Fresh ginger is now available in supermarkets across the country.

Herbs

There is not room in this book for an exhaustive discussion of herbs, but we can cover a few principles. Berkeley cooking relies heavily on the use of fresh herbs—the flavors of fresh herbs are truer and more interesting in general than those of their dried counterparts.

Sources: Dried herbs are available from supermarkets, delis, and gourmet markets, as well as the spice sections of many ethnic markets. Some produce markets carry fresh herbs, but the best source is your own garden. Most herbs are easy to grow and forgiving of mistakes. There is incomparable satisfaction in stepping out to your garden or even a few potted plants and snipping off a fresh sprig of this or that. Herbs make attractive borders, and you are assured of a supply of what are often scarce and expensive commodities. This is also a good way to slip into the very European (and very Berkeley) practice of keeping a kitchen garden, which might come to include your own patch of lettuces and baby vegetables.

Basil: Considered by some to be the queen of herbs, basil comes in a bewildering array of varieties in nurseries. The commercially grown sweet basil is the most widely used in cooking, however. There is nothing like fresh basil, especially not dried basil. Except for a pizza-bound tomato sauce or some Creole dishes, there is very little use for dried basil in Berkeley. We tend to go without during the winter, just to make that first plate of *pasta al pesto* taste better.

Bay Leaf: Use only the leaf of the Turkish bay laurel. This shrub grows well in mild climates and is said to do well indoors. Commercial dried bay leaves vary in quality. Look for leaves that still have some color and moisture.

Cilantro: Also known as Chinese parsley, this fragrant herb consists of the leaves of the coriander plant. Considered by some to be an acquired taste (mostly those who have yet to acquire the taste) cilantro is essential to authentic Mexican, Southeast Asian, Indian, Mideastern, and some Chinese cooking. Its delicate perfume completes the flavor combinations of garlic, ginger, spices, and, especially, chilies. *Sources*: Most produce markets, especially in Latin and Chinese neighborhoods.

Oregano and Marjoram: These cousins are widely confused and have many variants and subspecies and may be subspecies of each other. They look much alike; marjoram has reddish stems and small heart-shaped leaves and a perfumey, soapy fragrance. Oregano has darker stems, larger heart-shaped leaves and a fragrance reminiscent of pencil shavings. Neither fresh herb bears much resemblance to its dried form. Dried oregano is used in Mexican cooking and in Italian dishes. Dried marjoram is also used in Italian cooking, but it usually loses so much in the drying process that it might as well be left out.

Tarragon: This herb with its sweet licorice flavor is a French favorite and is well loved by many, although some people cannot bear it. It has been overused often, especially in its dried form, when it is stronger and less subtle than when fresh. Only French tarragon has the proper strength of flavor. If using dried tarragon, take care not to overdo it.

Thyme: The plant looks like a miniature evergreen shrub. It grows 12 to 18 inches high and has short dark-green needlelike leaves. There are many varieties, including silver, lemon, English, and creeping, and many "standard" types with confusing nomenclature. It is one of the most basic herbs, part of the traditional bouquet garni, and is used in stocks, as a poultry seasoning, and as an essential seasoning in many French dishes. This herb dries very well and quality brands are perfectly acceptable, although fresh thyme does have a nicer flavor.

Lemon Grass

Lemon grass looks like a large, coarse scallion and has the flavor and aroma of lemon without the tartness. It is used as a flavoring, like bay leaves, and not eaten by itself. *Sources*: Fresh lemon grass can be impossible to find in some parts of the country. Check in areas with Southeast Asian populations, or try asking at one of their restaurants. It is easy to grow; this is what most restaurants do. It is widely available in the Bay Area, in produce markets and in Chinatown. As a substitute for fresh lemon grass, use dried lemon grass tea, or check in an Indian grocery store for the powdered form, which may be called *"sereh poeder"* and is packaged by a Dutch exporter.

Mushrooms

From the pedestrian but serviceable *Agaricus bisporus* available commercially, to the seasonal boletuses, morels, and chanterelles, mushrooms have lent interest to the table for eons. Mushrooms of all types have recently become popular. It is now possible to buy fresh wild mushrooms in season at produce markets, as well as a wide variety of cultivated types.

Cultivated Mushrooms

In addition to the commercial mushrooms we have all used many times, growers are now producing a variety of Asian mushrooms. *Enoki*, or *straw mushrooms*, are tiny white fungi that grow in clumps and have an utterly charming appearance. They are used in salads and as a garnish and plate decoration, though their flavor contributes little. *Oyster mushrooms* are widespread wild mushrooms and one of the most successfully cultivated varieties. They grow on dead wood and are said to have a faint flavor of seafood. This is more true of the wild than the domestic variety. *Black forest*, or *shiitake*, mushrooms are another Asian type now widely cultivated. The fresh variety has excellent cooking characteristics, and it is refreshing to see a domesticated wild thing with such personality. *Sources*: Produce markets and supermarkets.

Wild Mushrooms

Now we enter the field of the arcane. While identification of most edible mushrooms is a simple matter, mistakes have dread implications. In the Bay Area, seasonal wild mushrooms are available in produce and gourmet markets, who procure them from proven sources.

Chanterelle: (*Cantherellus cibarius*) This beautiful mushroom is apricot yellow and aromatic, and is one of the choicest and easiest to identify of the wild mushrooms. They have a strong affinity for cream and white wine.

Field Mushroom: (*Agaricus campestris*) This mushroom is much like the commercial mushroom (which was bred from it), but has a characteristic "wild" flavor. It is tricky to identify because some of its close relatives cause stomach complaints in some people, and because in the button phase there is a danger of confusing it with a deadly amanita.

Morel: (*Morchella augusticeps, Morchella esculenta*) Considered by many to be the finest of wild mushrooms, the morel is also the easiest to identify, and one of the most expensive.

Cèpe: *(Boletus edulis)* Another very choice mushroom, available most often in the dried form and called *porcini*. It is the object of intense and secretive searching during the fall months after the rains begin. This mushroom is happiest combined with meats, game, red wine.

Dried Mushrooms

Morels, *porcini* (or *cèpes*), and *shiitake* mushrooms are most widely available in dried form. Drying accentuates and transforms mushroom flavors so that the dried product is really a different ingredient from the fresh. The shiitake, or black forest, mushroom is a basic ingredient in some Asian dishes, while the porcini, or cèpe, is used extensively in French and Italian cooking. Dried morels are used in the same way as cèpes, especially with game. *Sources:* Gourmet markets, Italian delis; at very high prices (fortunately, a little goes a long way). Shiitakes are available from Asian grocers and sometimes in the Oriental food sections of supermarkets.

Olive Oil

Talking about olive oil gets to be like talking about wine. The range and subtlety of the topic invite book-length discussion. Dating back to antiquity, olive oil has been a primary source of human nourishment. In its current use, it is still one of the most basic ingredients of Mediterranean cuisine and fits naturally into the "California-Mediterranean" style that characterizes much of our area's best cooking.

It takes at least two kinds of olive oil to stock your kitchen for the recipes in this book. First you should have a solid but not terribly expensive olive oil for basic cooking needs and as the base for many salad dressings and mayonnaises. The other olive oil you will need is one of the extra-virgin grade. This oil will be used mostly as a flavoring. Its delicate aromatic character suffers from cooking, while its strength can be overwhelming. And, of course, intermediate grades and strengths give the cook more flexibility. When buying the expensive olive oils, try a small bottle first. Also, unless they suit your taste, avoid dark or green olive oils; they can be very strong and acrid tasting. The preferred oil is extra-virgin grade, from Italy, France, Greece, Spain, or California. Price is not always the best indication of quality. Experiment—it's fun. *Sources:* Gourmet markets, Italian delicatessens, and even supermarkets carry olive oil. Supermarkets may be the cheapest places to buy quantities of standard-grade olive oil, but may not carry the fancier varieties.

Parmesan Cheese

There is only one kind of genuine Parmesan cheese, Parmigiano Reggiano. This cheese is strictly controlled by Italian law, aged at least eighteen months, and produced only three months of the year in a limited area of the country. It is handmade and necessarily expensive. At its best, when freshly cut from the wheel, it should be moist and grate easily, and should be served within minutes of grating. Store it well wrapped in your refrigerator and go ahead and use it within a couple of weeks. This absolutely extraordinary cheese makes an astounding difference in any dish calling for freshly grated cheese, and is vital to pastas, *risotti,* and a host of other Italian and California dishes. *Sources:* Italian grocers and gourmet markets.

Other Grating Cheeses
In this country "Parmesan cheese" has come to mean any aged, hard grating cheese, and some serviceable cheeses fall into this category The most important thing to know is that any cheese begins giving up its soul to the atmosphere as soon as it is grated. So never waste your money on pre-grated cheese. Buy the best-quality "Parmesan cheese" you can afford, by the chunk, and grate it yourself. The standard box-type cheese grater does an adequate job if you are grating just enough for a meal. Although not in the league of a Reggiano Parmesan, a good grade of domestic grating cheese will serve your needs until you can splurge on the real thing. In addition to the domestic version of Parmesan, there is a class of Italian cheeses called *grana,* which have more character and cost more than our domestic Parmesans. If you are going to cook the cheese, one of these lesser "Parmesans" will be more than adequate. *Sources:* Italian grocers, delicatessens, gourmet markets.

Sun-dried Tomatoes

This is currently a chic ingredient, and for good reason. The rich flavor of vine-ripened tomatoes acquires overtones of figs or raisins through the drying process. The tomatoes are split open lengthwise, salted, and dried in the sun in Southern Italy, where strings of drying tomatoes festoon the exteriors of many houses. After drying, the tomatoes are packed in olive oil or shipped dry, like dried fruit. Dried tomatoes are used in pastas, pizzas, sandwiches, and many other applications. *Sources:* Italian grocers, delicatessens, gourmet markets.

Tamarind

The pulp from the seed pod of a leguminous tree, tamarind is both tart and sweet. It is one of the flavors in cola drinks and is used as the basis of an Italian soda called *tamarindo*. It is also widely used in Mexican and South American cooking. The pulp is dark and gooey, almost gelatinous. To use the creature whole, peel the husk from the pod and extract the seeds from the pulp. Place the extracted pulp in a bowl or jar and cover it with boiling water, then let it soak for at least an hour. Then mash it together with your fingers and force the liquid through a sieve. And, yes, there is an easier way, which I found after several years of this struggle. Indian groceries carry a tamarind extract (Aeroplane brand) which is roughly the same strength as extracted tamarind pulp. And, for once, the processed product is as good as the natural one. *Sources:* Fresh whole tamarind can be found in the more complete produce markets, Asian stores, and Latino markets. The concentrate is available in Indian grocery stores.

Thai Perfumed Rice

This is another unfamiliar product, which after a heroic local search by Ruth Dorman was located in the community of San Pablo, California, in a tiny Vietnamese grocery store. It is a rice that is said to be scented with jasmine flowers. When cooked there is no hint of flowery aroma, but the rice is delicious: rich, fragrant, and nutty, unlike regular supermarket rice. It should be washed well and then cooked like any other white rice. *Sources:* Give yourself plenty of time and use the phone. Several grocers said they could order it for us, but then we would never have found that great little store. Perfumed rice is inexpensive, especially by the twenty-five-pound bag.

Wine for Cooking

It is said that the better the wine, the better the dish. There are definite limitations to this principle. While a fine aged Chardonnay will certainly spruce up your fish stock, it will do your table even more good. You might, though, in a moment of largesse or wealth, sacrifice a generous splash of that same jewel to the completion of a cream and white wine reduction and get a result almost worthy of the wine.

Here are a few rules of thumb concerning wine for cooking. The wine should almost always be dry, have at least medium body, and be young, with good solid acid content. In most cases there is no reason to spend a lot of money for it. For my taste, a good white wine for cooking is a young dry Chardonnay or a simple jug wine if the blend is not too heavy on the Semillon or Chenin Blanc grapes. For a red wine, I prefer a Zinfandel or, again, a dry red jug wine. For reductions of brown stock and red wine, especially for game or duck, nothing beats a young, robust, even coarse Zinfandel.

BASICS

TECHNIQUES
Buying and Storing Fish

Buying and storing fish are skills essential to any professional chef. The chef has a major advantage over the person shopping for the home table, because a day-to-day relationship with the supplier is carefully nurtured. The supplier understands the restaurant's needs and vice versa. The restaurant can always get fish that were bought that day at the wholesale market—fish that were, in most cases, caught only the day before, or even in the middle of the night.

The wholesale fish market is a rough place, and wholesalers do not hesitate to take advantage of the uninformed or careless buyer, which often means that a retailer may try to sell you his mistakes. A retailer also has to sell the fish left from the day before, which are sometimes just fine, although it is hard for the shopper to tell. So here are some guidelines.

1. When in doubt, ask. Which fish came in today? Tell the counterperson that your aged granny is allergic to seaborne bacteria and has to have the freshest fish or she'll die.

2. Learn to judge fish yourself. Through experience, it is possible to tell which fish are fresh on a given day and to estimate the approximate age of every fish in the counter. The freshest fish almost glow. Fish have a natural mucous coating, and this is what makes them shine when they are fresh. As the fish lies around in the walk-in or counter, the coating dries out and the fish looks dull. Do not go entirely by the appearance of the eyes. Fish are packed in crushed ice for shipping, and often the eyes freeze, causing them to appear dull. If the eyes are dull and sunken, though, that is an old fish. Go by the overall appearance of the fish and pay the most attention to the sheen of the fish. In buying fillets, which is what most domestic shoppers do, it is even harder to judge quality. The best rule is to go by the prettiness of the piece of fish. It should shine. It should beg you to buy it. You should think, "What a pretty piece of fish!"

3. Even though fish can be stored for up to five days, depending on the type of fish and its condition to start with, it is best to eat the fish the same day you buy it. If you must buy fish for tomorrow, wrap it tightly in plastic as soon as you get it home, and store it in the coldest place in your refrigerator (but not the freezer, silly). If you are storing whole fish, have the fish gutted and scaled, and, in either case, be extra demanding as to freshness.

Peeling and Using Garlic

In restaurants, large amounts of garlic are peeled at one time. The peeled garlic is stored in a container of oil and used as needed. It is important to seal garlic from contact with air as soon as it is peeled, because the flavor of garlic resides in certain volatile oils that oxidize on contact with the air, giving the garlic an acrid flavor.

You will find a wide range of garlic flavors used in this book. Because of the volatility of garlic's oils, different cooking techniques produce different flavors. Raw puréed garlic added to a dish at the last moment gives a strong, almost overpowering flavor, which is cherished in some dishes. At the other end of the scale is the sweet, subtle flavor of garlic that has been cooked for a long time at a low temperature, such as baked garlic or garlic simmered in a stock or stew. And in between we have the potent flavor of garlic browned in oil, and the rich flavor of garlic sautéed briefly and then simmered with the rest of a dish. As you can see, we have a lot of fun with garlic here. Life just wouldn't be the same without it.

To peel garlic restaurant style, remove the outer layers of loose parchmentlike stuff from a whole head of garlic. Put the head of garlic on its side on a hard surface, rest the heel of your right hand on it, cover your right hand with the left and lean forward, putting most of your weight on the head of garlic. It will separate into cloves. Next, with a kitchen mallet or the flat of a cleaver, crush the cloves lightly; they should be cracked open, not mashed flat. Pick up each clove by the pointed end, pinch it between your fingers, and, with your other hand, twist the clove out of its husk and drop it into a small container of oil. (You might as well peel another head; it keeps for weeks in the refrigerator.)

Grilling

This is one of the most important techniques used in our area, arguably the most influential development in American cooking in years. Silly, of course—man has been burning his dinner over an open fire for eons. But it became newly popular here, and led to a style of simplicity in cooking that took off like a Chez Panisse mesquite shed on fire.

Fuels for Grilling

Mesquite is all the vogue for grilling, and for good reason. Commercial charcoal briquets may have the advantages of price and easier-to-control heat, but they impart a flavor of petroleum to the food, which is easy to understand since they are composed mostly of petroleum wastes. Mesquite burns with an intense heat, which is at times a blessing and at others a curse. It works beautifully for fish, but it can set a grill full of split chickens afire. The covered barbecue grill is the answer to this problem, for it allows the cook to control the amount of air the fire gets and therefore how much fire there is to be. *Gas* is another fuel used both in restaurants and at home, and while there is nothing wrong with it, there is also nothing to recommend it, as it adds no flavor of its own to the food.

The most underestimated fuel, in my opinion, is also the oldest: *wood*. It is the very definition of organic, has lots of character, and is no more expensive than charcoal—in fact it's often free. While it may take certain woodsmanly skills to kindle the fire, there is a primitive satisfaction in doing so.

While starting your charcoal or wood fire Boy Scout style does avoid the unpleasant and probably poisonous odors of charcoal lighter, there are at least two easier ways. One is with a chimney device that holds a few pieces of charcoal or wood. You wad up one piece of newspaper, place it underneath, light it, and the chimney funnels the heat through the fuel, igniting it rapidly. You then build your fire around those few lit pieces. The other method is an electric lighting coil, which you pile charcoal around and leave on for about 10 minutes. Both methods work well, and the chimney lighter is very inexpensive.

Roasting and Peeling Peppers

This is an age-old procedure. Roasting and peeling peppers greatly enhances their sweetness and mellows their flavors. While there are many techniques, the principles are the same: application of some kind of heat to the skin to loosen it from the meat, a period of steaming and cooling, then removal of the skin. The easiest method I know is to char the skin of the pepper over an open flame, either gas or charcoal. This takes about 5 minutes and should result in a pepper that is almost completely black (yes, black). The hot pepper is then put into a paper bag, which is folded closed, and the pepper is left to cool. The charred skin is either scraped or rinsed off (purists insist on scraping, maintaining that rinsing causes flavor loss), then the pepper is stemmed, seeded, and cut as desired, for most dishes into long narrow strips.

RECIPES
Beurre Blanc

Beurre blanc is one member of a large family of hot butter sauces. These sauces are formed by the emulsification of butterfat with the milk solids and water of butter by the action of a strongly acid, usually flavored, reduction. In practice what happens is that an acid liquid such as wine vinegar or lemon juice is reduced over medium heat with flavorings such as wine, shallots, or herbs to an almost syrupy consistency, just a tablespoon or so in volume. Then, over low heat, cold butter is melted into the reduction, whose very acid nature binds the fatty components with the watery elements of the butter, forming what is called an emulsion and which has an attractive, creamy appearance. Butter continues to be melted into the sauce until the acid balance tastes correct. The beginner should do this process over low heat, but the experienced professional can do it over a roaring flame.

Here is a basic beurre blanc recipe. Bear in mind that it can be flavored in any way desired, as long as the basic architecture of the sauce is honored.

¼ cup white wine vinegar
¼ cup fresh lemon juice
¼ cup dry white wine
2 tablespoons minced shallots
2 cups (4 sticks) cold unsalted butter, cut into 12 pieces

In a heavy, nonreactive saucepan (enameled or stainless steel), boil the shallots and liquids until only a tablespoon or so remains. Remove the saucepan from the heat and immediately stir in 2 pieces of cold butter. As the butter melts and is incorporated, return the pan to a low flame and add the rest of the butter a piece at a time, stirring constantly. As you approach the end of the butter, taste the sauce to make sure it will be neither too acid nor too bland. Once the sauce is complete, it may be kept in a very warm, but not hot, place for several hours.

If you do something wrong, such as using warm or melted butter or too much heat, and the sauce "breaks" or turns thin and oily, it may be recovered in one of two ways: Make a small amount of a new reduction, add more cold butter, and then add the broken sauce gradually to that, or whisk a small amount of the broken sauce in a mixing bowl with a small piece of ice, then work in the broken sauce. In my experience, the first method works more reliably.

To vary the sauce, add herbs to simmer with the reduction or after the sauce is complete. The sauce may be flavored with chopped fresh tomatoes, garlic, chilies, or spices. Or you may use all lemon juice and omit the vinegar, or use orange or another fruit juice. There are no limits so long as there is enough

acid to make the sauce hold together. Stocks may also be reduced along with the vinegar; fish stock and tarragon, for example, is a simple variation of the basic recipe.

Composed Butters

These are flavored butters. Good-quality unsalted butter is softened, and then a concentrated flavor of some kind is introduced, for instance a reduction of orange juice and garlic, or lime juice, lime zest, and ground coriander. The butter is then shaped as desired—usually into a roll about 2 inches in diameter—chilled, and served over hot grilled foods.

Stocks

Restaurants make extensive use of stocks, and so does this book. Stocks form the basis for so many flavors and techniques that a chef is lost without at least three on hand at all times. The making of stock is so simple that the recipe is almost just a concept: clean bones and leftovers simmered in water with or without flavorings until their essence is extracted. It should be remembered that stocks freeze well, can be made in large quantity, and require relatively little of the cook's time, so it is easy to guarantee that you will never be without them. (To store them in the refrigerator, bring to a boil every 3 or 4 days.) If you do get caught short, it is possible to buy stocks in some delicatessens. As a last resort, canned broths are available and can be made to resemble the real thing by simmering them with some carrots, celery, onions, etc., as well as whatever meat or fish scraps you may have around. Dehydrated bouillon cubes or soup bases do more harm than good. They have a phony flavor that no amount of adjusting can disguise.

The same rules apply to materials for stock as to ingredients in general: Freshness and cleanliness are paramount. We will discuss the three basic stocks: chicken stock, fish stock and brown stock. For *chicken (or duck) stock*, use bones, (raw or cooked), skin, fat, and leftover meat. Any one or any combination of these is fine. The raw components must be washed thoroughly. For *fish stock*, use bones, heads and meat only; never use the fins, tail, or skin. These contain oils that give stock a fishy taste. The parts for fish stock must be washed clean of all blood and slime, which usually takes three rinsings in cold water. For *brown stock*, use beef, veal, or pork bones and meat and scraps, or a mixture (brown poultry stock can be made with the same ingredients). Veal bones contain lots of gelatin, which gives the stock body and is important if the stock is to be reduced to a glaze. The material for brown stock can be trimmed of fat before cooking; this simplifies the skimming process. Bones for brown stock should not be washed, because this slows the browning process. In a large roasting pan, arrange the bones in one layer and roast them in a 500° oven until they are well browned, but not burned. This will take about an hour for beef bones, and about half an hour for poultry. With tongs, remove the bones to a large pot and pour off the grease from the roasting pan, reserving it if desired. Rinse out the pan and add the deglazing to the stock.

The simmering process is identical for all stocks, the only variable being cooking time.

Stock should be cooked in a large nonreactive pot; aluminum discolors it. Place the bones in the pot and add generous quantities of aromatic vegetables: onions, carrots, celery, parsley stems, garlic, and herbs. This is the point at which you can flavor the stock according to your intentions. The vegetables for brown stock can be used raw, browned with the bones, or sautéed. Cold water should be added to cover the stock material by at least 2 inches, and then the pot goes over a high flame. As it approaches boiling, blood and other impurities will begin to be cooked out and will rise to the surface as a foam. Hover resolutely over the pot for the next 10 minutes or so, skimming carefully with a large spoon or shallow ladle. Do not let the stock reach an actual boil. It should only simmer; that is, occasional bubbles will rise to the top. You should never stir a stock, but it is acceptable to jostle the bones gently to dislodge bits of scum that get hung up and don't float up to the surface. When the stock stops sending up foam, you are basically done skimming. An occasional visit to remove excess fat will be sufficient.

Cooking times vary. Fish stock is usually done in an hour or less. Chicken stock is best after 8 hours. A brown duck stock likes to cook about 24 hours, and a brown beef, veal, or lamb stock should really cook for 3 days. If you are in a hurry, cook the stock as long as you can and then call it done. Let the stock cool in the pot, then ladle it out through a strainer lined with layers of cheesecloth or a kitchen towel, and finally pour out the last liquid from the pot when it gets too far down to use the ladle.   PTJ

Compliments of
the Chef

For years a Berkeley standby in the realm of classic French cooking, A La Carte was one of the first restaurants in town to offer an à la carte menu allowing diners to compose their own meal according to taste and budget. Located near an unlikely corner in a residential neighborhood, this tiny restaurant, with its enormous fireplace, ornate plasterwork, and starched pink linens, conveys a feeling of quiet intimacy.

Compliments of

A LA CARTE
BERKELEY

Suprême de Volaille en Feuilletée

Chicken Breast in Puff Pastry

This rich main dish is a bit tricky; if your pastry does not puff using the technique given here, try using a crêpe as a base for the stuffed chicken breast and folding the puff pastry over all.

½ cup *each* minced fresh chives and dill
1 cup minced fresh parsley
½ cup chopped fresh chervil
¼ cup chopped garlic
1½ pounds natural cream cheese
Salt and pepper
2 pounds puff pastry
8 whole chicken breasts, skinned and boned but left whole
1 egg yolk mixed with
1 tablespoon heavy cream

Cream the herbs and garlic together with the cream cheese. Season to taste with salt and pepper and set aside. Roll out the puff pastry ¼ to ⅛ inch thick. Cut into eight 6- by 10-inch rectangles. Place approximately 3 tablespoons of the herbed cream cheese filling on each breast and fold the meat over it, taking care not to overfill.

Place the filled breast on a piece of pastry and fold the pastry over the meat loosely so that it will have room to puff. Seal the edges, chill for 1 hour, and place seam side down and well apart on an ungreased cookie sheet. Brush with the egg-cream mixture. Bake in a preheated 400° oven for 20 to 30 minutes, or until golden brown. *Serves 8.*

Pots de Crème au Chocolat Grand Marnier

Chocolate Custard Cream

A rich and satisfying dessert, easy to execute.

2⅔ cups plus ½ cup heavy cream
8 ounces (8 squares) fine bittersweet baking chocolate
8 large egg yolks
8 tablespoons sugar
1 tablespoon vanilla extract
¼ cup plus dash Grand Marnier liqueur
Powdered sugar
Chocolate shavings (optional)

Pour 2⅔ cups of the cream into a heavy saucepan over low heat. Add the chocolate and melt, stirring occasionally; do not boil. In a large bowl, beat the egg yolks into the sugar with a whisk until well mixed. Slowly, to avoid scrambling the yolks, pour the chocolate-cream mixture into the egg-sugar mixture, whisking to blend well. Add the vanilla and ¼ cup of the Grand Marnier and mix well.

Pour into 8 ungreased 4-ounce custard cups and place in a roasting pan with ½ inch of water covering the bottom. Bake in a preheated 200° oven for 1 hour, or until the top is slightly firm to the touch (your finger should not leave an imprint). Chill 1 hour.

To serve, whip the remaining ½ cup cream with a sprinkle of powdered sugar and a dash of Grand Marnier. Place a spoonful on top of each custard and add chocolate shavings, if desired. *Serves 8.*

A focus on pasta and grilled fish is the hallmark of this restaurant. Grilled foods are accompanied with simple sauces, the pasta and seafood are absolutely fresh, and the menu changes daily. Owner Bonnie Hughes has managed to incorporate a Continental flavor into quintessential California cuisine. Displays of antipasti and desserts greet diners as they enter the lower dining room, where tables are arranged around a central fireplace. The partially open kitchen dominates the upper, more casual dining room, with a large enclosed garden dining area beyond.

Once a year Augusta's presents an entire meal devoted to "unmentionable cuisine" including, among other offerings, snake and conch. Although the less adventurous may choose to forego this experience, enthusiastic diners have included food writers and cooks from all over California.

Compliments of

AUGUSTA'S
BERKELEY

Caesar Salad

One of the best renditions of a popular Berkeley salad. A meal by itself on a hot summer day, it is also an ideal beginner for a menu based on grilled food. Always use freshly grated Parmesan cheese for a Caesar salad, Reggiano if possible.

Croutons

½-inch-thick slices of day-old French bread or
   quarter-inch slices of day-old baguette,
   cubed (enough to make ¾ cups of croutons)
Olive oil
1 or 2 garlic cloves, minced

2 eggs
1 large head romaine lettuce
3 tablespoons fresh lemon juice, or more to
   taste
¾ cup olive oil
1 garlic clove, minced
¼ teaspoon Worcestershire sauce
2 tablespoons chopped anchovies
⅓ cup freshly grated Parmesan cheese

Prepare croutons by toasting the cubed bread in a preheated 300° oven for 30 minutes, or until lightly brown and completely dry. Drizzle with olive oil and some minced garlic and toast another 5 minutes. Set aside. (These will keep for several days in a sealed container. Do not refrigerate.)

   Coddle the 2 eggs in boiling water for 30 seconds. Tear the lettuce into bite-sized pieces. Beat the eggs well. Combine the lemon juice, oil, and garlic and mix well. Gradually whisk in the eggs, forming an emulsion. Add the Worcestershire and anchovies. Toss with the lettuce, Parmesan, and croutons. Garnish with additional Parmesan if desired. *Serves 2 to 4.*

Roast Garlic Potatoes

This simple and very popular dish is an obvious choice to serve with steaks, roasts, or any other uncomplicated dish. The amount of garlic may be adjusted to your taste, and olive oil is a good substitute for clarified butter. Other types of potatoes also work well. After baking, the garlic becomes soft and sweet and is squeezed out of the husk to flavor each bite of potato.

4 medium russet potatoes
Salt and ground white pepper to taste
24 whole unpeeled garlic cloves
   (less or more if desired)
½ cup clarified butter or olive oil

Cut the potatoes in half and then cut each half into thirds. Put the potatoes, skin side down, in an oiled baking pan. Sprinkle with salt and white pepper. Add the whole cloves of garlic (with their skins) on top of the potatoes. Drizzle the clarified butter or olive oil on top. Bake in a preheated 375° oven for 30 to 45 minutes. To prepare ahead, reheat at 450° for 10 minutes. They will be brown, slightly puffed, and ready to serve immediately; they will not wait. *Serves 4.*

Tomato, Basil, and Pine Nut Fettuccine

A pasta that is easy on the cook, and great for a quick meal or as a first course in an elaborate menu. Roasting the tomatoes dries them out and gives them a special flavor. Roma, or plum, tomatoes work best because of their lower moisture content.

3 tablespoons pine nuts
2 pounds tomatoes, cored and cut into
  wedges
3 tablespoons olive oil
Salt and pepper to taste
Small handful basil leaves
2 tablespoons minced garlic
¼ cup white wine
¼ cup chicken stock
½ tablespoon dried red pepper flakes
½ pound fresh pasta
Freshly grated Parmesan

Toast the pine nuts for 10 minutes in a preheated 300° oven. Roast the tomatoes in a 400° oven with 1 tablespoon of the olive oil, salt, and pepper, until the skins are slightly browned. Chop the basil coarsely. Sauté the garlic in the remaining 2 tablespoons of olive oil. Add the tomatoes, pine nuts, and basil. Add the wine and stock and cook until slightly reduced. Season with red pepper flakes.

Cook the pasta in lots of salted boiling water until *al dente*, 2 to 3 minutes. Mix a little sauce into the freshly cooked pasta and pour the rest over the top. Serve with grated Parmesan. *Serves 4.*

Sautéed Swordfish with Tomato and Dill Sauce

Sautéed swordfish with tomato and dill sauce is a quick and easy dish. Fresh dill makes all the difference here. Sweet cream may be used instead of crème fraîche, but a few drops of lemon juice should be added to simulate the tang of crème fraîche.

2 swordfish steaks, 6 to 8 ounces each
1 tablespoon clarified butter
1 teaspoon minced garlic
1 tablespoon peeled, seeded, and chopped
  tomato
¼ cup dry white wine
½ cup crème fraîche
1 teaspoon chopped fresh dill
4 tablespoons butter
Salt and pepper
Lemon wedges
Sprigs of dill

In a sauté pan or skillet, gently sauté the swordfish in the clarified butter until just done, about 3 to 5 minutes per side, depending on the thickness of the steaks (the fish should be slightly translucent in the center). Remove from the pan and keep warm.

Add the garlic, tomato, and wine to the pan and reduce until almost dry. Add the crème fraîche and reduce by one-third to one-half. Remove from the heat. Add the dill. Add the butter, stirring until it melts and is incorporated into the sauce. Season to taste with salt and pepper and pour over the swordfish. Garnish with lemon wedges and dill. *Serves 2.*

Compliments of

BAY WOLF
RESTAURANT
OAKLAND

*F*or a restaurant that began as a cheese shop and cafe, the Bay Wolf has come far. It was created by former academics Michael Wild, Larry Goldman, and Michael Phelps (the name of the restaurant is a literary pun). Now Wild and Carol Brendlinger have developed the Bay Wolf into one of the most respected restaurants in the Bay Area. It is located in a Victorian house with detailed woodwork, etched glass, and a handsome bar. A large outdoor dining deck overlooks the busy scene on Piedmont Avenue.

The Bay Wolf features an eclectic French menu that changes daily, and even the most frequent patrons are unlikely to anticipate some of the imaginative combinations devised in this kitchen. Michael Wild, harking back to his childhood in Provence, has evolved a unique style of California cuisine based on French country cooking modified by Creole and Mideastern influences. The management of the Bay Wolf is also unusual: many of the decisions are made by the staff, and this group participation is reflected in the high quality of the food and friendliness of the service.

Giblet Soup with Barley, Garlic, and Mushrooms

A robust soup, created by Michael Wild, that could stand alone as a meal or could serve to introduce a roast of fowl. If you plan to serve it the following day, have some stock on hand to dilute it, as the barley soaks up moisture over time.

2 ounces dried *porcini* mushrooms
1 quart poultry stock
Salt to taste
⅓ cup barley
1 garlic clove, chopped
1 pound giblets, trimmed and finely diced
¾ pound fresh mushrooms, domestic or wild
1 garlic clove, minced
2 celery stalks, minced
1 medium onion, minced
3 green onions, sliced thin
6 parsley sprigs, chopped
4 tablespoons peanut oil or rendered chicken, duck, or goose fat

Gremolata

6 garlic cloves
1 bunch parsley
Zest of 2 lemons

Soak the porcini in hot water to cover for 1 hour; drain the mushrooms, reserving the soaking liquid. Place the poultry stock in a large saucepan, salt lightly, add the barley, and simmer about 45 minutes, or until tender. Add the chopped garlic to the broth. In a large, heavy pot, sauté the giblets, fresh

mushrooms, garlic, celery, onions, and parsley in the oil until pleasantly aromatic and nearly tender. Add the cooked barley and stock and mushroom soaking liquid; simmer for 15 minutes.

Prepare the *gremolata* by mincing the garlic, parsley, and lemon zest together with a chef's knife or in a food processor. Serve the soup with the gremolata on the side. *Serves 4 to 6.*

Spinach Salad with Duck Cracklings

This recipe came from a menu by Michael Wild, which used a different part of the duck for every course of the meal, except dessert. Duck cracklings make this an interesting and successful variation of spinach salad.

Skin from 3 duck breasts
1 lemon cucumber or English or Japanese cucumber
2 bunches spinach leaves, stemmed
⅓ cup grape juice or Gamay verjuice
2 tablespoons fresh lemon juice
⅜ cup olive oil
1 shallot, minced
Salt and pepper to taste

Place the duck skin on a rack in a pan in a preheated 375° oven for 45 minutes, or until the skin is crisp and browned, but not too brown. (A convection oven works well for this.) Save the fat for other cooking. Crack the skin into small pieces and drain on paper towels.

Peel, seed, and julienne the cucumber. Add to the spinach and toss with a dressing made by combining the grape juice or verjuice, lemon juice, olive oil, shallot, salt, and pepper. Sprinkle the salad with the cracklings and serve immediately. *Serves 4 to 6.*

Pumpkin Ravioli with Crème Fraîche and Chives

*A*n *unusual first course for an elaborate meal or a main course for a simple one, these raviolis, created by Carol Brendlinger, lend themselves beautifully to variation. The simple addition of a variety of fresh herbs to the pumpkin purée makes an already excellent dish even more interesting. Favorite additions are mint, marjoram, and basil. Imagination, discretion, and the rest of the menu are the only limitations.*

Canned pumpkin can be used, but fresh is better. To cook it, steam or bake peeled pumpkin slices until tender and drain well to prevent the filling from being too wet. If pumpkin is not available, use butternut squash or another winter squash. The raviolis do not hold or freeze well, as they tend to stick together. And take care with the sauce, which curdles easily (although it will still taste fine).

Filling

1 cup fresh pumpkin purée, well drained
1 egg, beaten
¼ pound cheese (grated Gruyère or Parmesan, or crumbled *chèvre*)

¼ cup minced fresh chives
¼ teaspoon salt
¼ teaspoon ground white pepper

½ pound fresh pasta cut into 4-inch-wide sheets.

Sauce

2 cups *crème fraîche*
4 egg yolks
½ teaspoon grated lemon zest
¼ teaspoon salt
Pinch of ground white pepper
¼ cup minced fresh chives

Mix the ingredients for the filling together. Make a row of teaspoonfuls of the filling 2 inches apart along one side of the pasta sheets. Fold each sheet in half lengthwise, moistening the dough around the filling with water to make it stick together. Press to seal, pushing out any air bubbles. Cut into squares with a ravioli wheel. Cook in a large amount of boiling salted water for 2 to 5 minutes (depending on thickness of pasta) or until *al dente.*

Meanwhile, prepare the sauce by mixing all the sauce ingredients in the top of a double boiler. Heat slowly over simmering water, whisking constantly, until the sauce thickens. Drain the ravioli in a colander. Pour the sauce over the ravioli and serve immediately. *Serves 6 as a main course, 12 as an appetizer.*

Duck Sausage Wrapped in Grape Leaves with Zinfandel Sauce

Another magnificent dish from Bay Wolf's all-duck menu is this most unusual sausage, involving neither pork nor sausage casing. A meat grinder is preferable to a food processor for this recipe because the processor cannot cut the tendinous material that runs through the meat of the duck leg.

Four-spices, or quatre-épices, *is a blend of one part each clove, nutmeg, and ginger to three parts cinnamon (you can substitute allspice).*

Sausage

Fresh or canned grape leaves
6 boned duck legs, uncooked
1 shallot
2 to 3 garlic cloves
Salt and pepper to taste
½ teaspoon four-spices (see introductory note)
Pinch dried red pepper flakes
1 cup duck stock or rich chicken stock

Sauce

2 quarts duck stock or rich chicken stock
Reserved braising liquid
1 bottle Zinfandel

If the grape leaves are fresh, blanch first in salted water for 10 minutes before wrapping. Put the duck meat through a meat grinder with the shallot, garlic, and spices. Mix well, divide into 12 portions, and wrap in the grape leaves. Pour the duck or chicken stock into a pan large enough to hold all of the sausages. Braise in a preheated 400° oven for 30 minutes or cook on a covered charcoal grill. In either case, reserve the braising liquid to use in the sauce.

To make the sauce, combine the stock and Zinfandel in a pan and reduce to a syrupy sauce. (You can flavor the reduction, if you like, with tomato, garlic, onion, thyme, *herbes de Provence*, and small amounts of celery and carrot.) Pour the sauce over the sausage. Garnish with polenta that has been cooked, cooled in a flat pan, cut into shapes with a cookie cutter, and grilled or sautéed. *Serves 6 as an entrée, 10 to 12 as an appetizer.*

For those of us who remember, entering Bette's is like stepping into a '57 Chevy Bel Air. Bette's is a lively eighties version of a fifties diner, complete with jukebox, rotating counter stools covered in vinyl, clean-lined chrome trim, and Fiestaware crockery. The updated American menu features some Mexican influences, and the food is both hearty and imaginative. The crowd is diverse, and on any visit you are likely to encounter exercise buffs from the studio next door as well as businessmen in three-piece suits enjoying the excellent food and upbeat atmosphere.

Huevos Rancheros

Ranch-Style Eggs

What more could you want for breakfast than spicy beans, tortillas, and fried eggs topped with melted cheese and salsa? Make sure to cook the beans long enough so that they begin to melt into a creamy purée, adding water as needed to prevent scorching. The sauce and bean recipes make enough for six to eight servings; the Huevos Rancheros recipe instructions are for one serving.

2 eggs
Butter for frying
½ cup Salsa, following
¼ cup shredded Cheddar cheese
¼ cup shredded jack cheese
1 flour tortilla
Black Beans, following
1 tablespoon sour cream

In a small shallow ovenproof pan, cook the eggs sunnyside up in a little butter until set on bottom but loose on top. Spoon ¼ cup salsa onto the eggs and top with shredded Cheddar and jack cheese to cover. Place the pan under the broiler until the cheese melts. Warm a flour tortilla in a sauté pan or skillet in a little butter. Slide the eggs onto the tortilla. Serve immediately with black beans topped with the remaining salsa and the sour cream. *Serves 1.*

Black Beans

1 pound dried black beans
1 medium yellow onion, minced
1 tablespoon ground cumin
1 tablespoon ground coriander
½ teaspoon cayenne
2 tablespoons olive oil
2 garlic cloves, minced
½ cup fresh orange juice
1 tablespoon salt
Ground pepper to taste

Soak the beans overnight in water to cover. In a sauté pan or skillet, sauté the onion, cumin, coriander, and cayenne in the olive oil until the onions are translucent. Add water to 2 inches above the surface of the beans. Combine the water and beans with the onion mixture in a heavy pot and simmer, uncovered, until the beans are soft and a thick sauce forms, about 2 hours. Add the garlic, orange juice, salt, pepper, and more water if necessary. Simmer another 30 minutes, stirring. *Makes about 6 cups.*

Salsa

6 to 8 ripe tomatoes, diced
1 bunch green onions, minced
2 fresh *jalapeño* peppers, diced
    (for a milder dish, stem and seed the peppers)
1 tablespoon salt
2 shakes Tabasco sauce
2 tablespoons butter

Simmer the tomatoes, green onions, jalapeños, salt, Tabasco, and butter in a saucepan until the liquid is reduced and the tomatoes have cooked down to the consistency of a loose purée. *Makes 3 to 4 cups.*

NOTE: This sauce will keep in the refrigerator for about a week.

German-Style Potato Pancakes

These pancakes are versatile enough to be served as a side dish for most meats, and they are excellent for breakfast as well.

1 small onion, grated
2 eggs, well beaten
¼ cup unbleached all-purpose flour
Salt and pepper to taste
6 medium russet potatoes, peeled
Shortening

Combine the grated onion, eggs, flour, salt, and pepper in a large mixing bowl and beat until the batter is smooth. Shred the potatoes on the big holes of a hand grater. Squeeze the potatoes in a clean tea towel until they are as dry as possible. Add the potatoes to the batter.

In a large sauté pan or skillet, melt shortening to the depth of ¼ inch. When it is hot but not smoking, spoon in mounds of potatoes and flatten into pancakes with the back of a spatula. When the pancakes are golden brown on the bottom, turn and press with the spatula again. Cook until golden brown and crisp. Remove from the pan with a slotted spatula and drain on paper towels. Serve hot with applesauce, sour cream, jam or sugar. *Serves 6.*

Souffléed Apple Pancake

This is just the dish for a special brunch, and it would make a nice dessert with the addition of a little more sugar and a fruit sauce. The apples can be replaced by bananas, berries, or other fruits in season.

2 green apples
4 tablespoons butter
¼ teaspoon ground cinnamon
2 teaspoons sugar
¾ cup half and half
½ cup unbleached all-purpose flour
¼ teaspoon salt
3 eggs, separated
4 tablespoons melted butter
2 tablespoons rum or brandy

Peel and slice the apples. In a sauté pan or skillet, sauté the apple slices lightly in 2 tablespoons of the butter, and add the cinnamon and sugar. Set aside. Combine the half and half, flour, and salt in a mixing bowl. Beat the egg yolks lightly and add to batter, then add the melted butter and the rum or brandy. Beat the egg whites until they form soft peaks. Fold the batter into them.

In an ovenproof skillet, heat the remaining 2 tablespoons of butter until it foams. Add the batter and cook briefly over medium heat. Arrange the apples on the top and continue cooking until the bottom is golden brown and bubbles form around the edge of the pancake. Place the pan under a preheated broiler until the middle is firm and the top is golden brown and puffed. *Serves 2.*

In the restaurant business success and expansion go hand in hand. The crowds at Bette's Diner inspired the owners, Bette and Manfred Kroening and Sue Conley, to open a deli and bakery next door. Chef Carolyn Weil, formerly in charge of pastry at Stars and the Santa Fe Grill, produces wonderful food to go (including dozens of innovative salads, hot foods, and pizzas), oversees a complete bakery, and even makes her own yogurt.

Compliments of

BETTE'S-TO-GO
BERKELEY

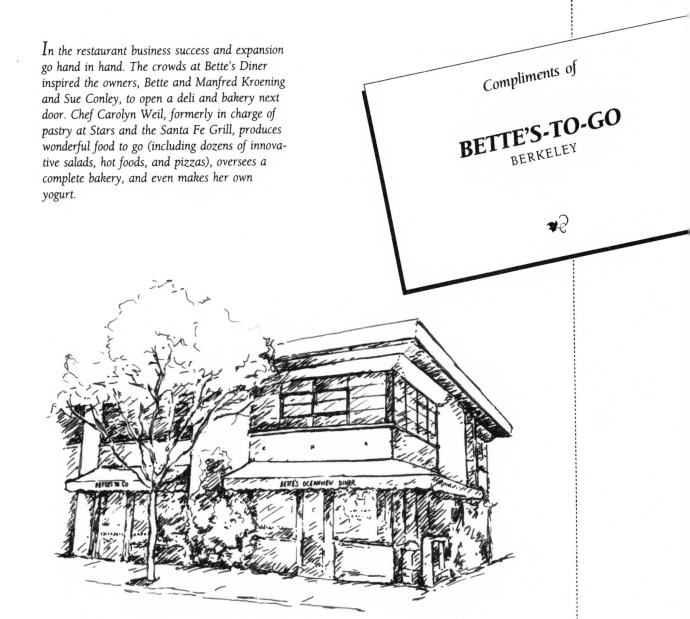

Chinese Chicken Salad

*T*his is probably the most popular salad at
Bette's-To-Go. The dressing keeps well, even im-
proving with time, and the quantities given are
sufficient for two salads.

Dressing

½ cup dark sesame oil
¾ cup corn or peanut oil
⅓ cup soy sauce
⅓ cup rice vinegar
¼ cup brown sugar
⅛ cup cider vinegar
2 tablespoons fresh ginger, minced
1 teaspoon red pepper flakes
6 cloves garlic, minced

Salad

2 whole chicken breasts (4 boneless fillets),
   with skin left on
Olive or vegetable oil
1 cup snow peas
2 cucumbers, cut in half rounds (peeled and
   seeded if domestic)
2 red bell peppers, julienned
1 bunch scallions, julienned
¼ cup roasted peanuts, chopped
Cilantro

Combine the ingredients for the dressing and
allow to stand while preparing the salad.
   Cook the chicken in a hot heavy skillet in a
small quantity of oil until just done. When it
cools, cut in ½-inch strips, with or without
the skin, according to taste.

Blanch the snow peas very briefly in boiling
water and douse immediately with cold
water to stop cooking and set the color. Dry
thoroughly.
   Combine the salad ingredients and about
half of the dressing. Mix the dressing well before using, and use more or less according to
taste. Garnish with cilantro leaves. *Serves 6.*

Mexican Chicken Salad

This is a hearty salad with vibrant colors and flavors.

2 whole chicken breasts (4 boneless fillets),
  with skin left on.
Olive or vegetable oil
⅔ cup uncooked corn, cut off the cob
⅔ cup black-eyed peas, soaked overnight and
  cooked until just tender
⅔ cup cooked rice
⅔ cup red bell pepper, julienned
⅔ cup red onion, julienned
2 teaspoons *pasilla* chili powder
Cilantro
Lime wedges

Vinaigrette

¼ cup red wine vinegar
2 tablespoons Dijon mustard
2 cloves garlic, minced
Salt and freshly ground pepper to taste
¾ cup olive oil

To make the vinaigrette, combine the vinegar, mustard, garlic, and salt. Whisk in the oil and set aside.

Cook the chicken in a small quantity of oil in a hot heavy pan until just done. When the chicken cools, cut it in ½-inch strips, with or without the skin, according to taste. Combine all the salad ingredients, and dress with the vinaigrette. Garnish with cilantro leaves and lime wedges. *Serves 6.*

Bombay Cuisine is one of Berkeley's small restaurant treasures. A single dining room done in pink and glass is overseen by the owners, the Parmar brothers. A recent addition to a miraculously complete Indian grocery store, Bombay Cuisine serves a number of dishes never seen on the menus of more formal, northern Indian restaurants, and we offer two of them here.

Khaman Dhokla

Yellow Split-Pea "Cornbread"

This dish can be considered a triumph of vegetarian cookery. It relies on principles and techniques foreign to the West and the results are wonderful. A batter of ground yellow split peas, split-pea flour, and flavorings is left to ferment overnight, then steamed. To avoid a jolting culture shock, guests should be warned that, despite appearances, this really is not cornbread.

1 cup *chana dal* (ground yellow split peas)
¼ cup *chana basen* (split-pea flour)
1 cup buttermilk
1 teaspoon ginger, peeled and chopped
1 hot green chili, or to taste
1½ teaspoons salt
¼ teaspoon ground turmeric
¼ cup vegetable oil
1 teaspoon Eno (an Indian brand of baking powder) or regular baking powder

Waghar

2 tablespoons vegetable oil
1 teaspoon black mustard seeds

Garnish

1 teaspoon ground unsweetened coconut
1 tablespoon chopped fresh cilantro

Soak the chana dal for 4 hours in 1 cup of water. If all the water is absorbed, add a little more.

In a blender or food processor, grind the dal with the buttermilk, chana basen, ginger, green chili, salt, turmeric, and oil. Cover loosely and leave overnight to ferment.

The next day, add a teaspoon of Eno or regular baking powder, place the batter in a shallow baking dish, and steam for 15 minutes, or until the Dhokla is firm and tests done by leaving no residue when pierced with a straw or knife.

When cool, make the Waghar by heating the mustard seeds until they turn dark and give off a smoky aroma. Be careful doing this: the seeds often pop and splatter. Pour the oil and seeds over the Dhokla, garnish with coconut and cilantro, and serve with Green Chutney, following. *Serves 4.*

Green Chutney

½ cup ground unsweetened coconut
1 inch fresh ginger, peeled and roughly chopped
1½ teaspoons sugar
2 tablespoons lemon or lime juice
4 or 5 mild green chilies, or to taste
2 bunches cilantro
Salt to taste

Grind all the ingredients together in a blender or food processor, adding a little water to keep things moving.

Onion Uthapa

Onion Pancake

This Indian appetizer looks like an onion pizza and, though intended to be served with soup and chutney, would be at home as a part of an array of finger foods or go well alongside a spicy lamb dish.

1 cup rice
¼ cup *urad dal* (black-husked lentil)
⅛ cup red lentils
½ teaspoon salt
Pinch baking powder
1½ cups water

Topping

2 medium onions, chopped
1 teaspoon ground cumin
1 pinch *hing* (asafoetida)
½ teaspoon salt
2 teaspoons chopped cilantro
½ teaspoon chopped green chilies

Soak the rice, urad dal, and red lentils in water for 4 hours. Then, in a blender or food processor, grind into a batter. Add water if necessary to obtain a purée the thickness of pancake batter. Add the salt and baking powder and place the batter, covered loosely, in a warm place overnight to ferment.

To make the topping, mix together the onions, spices, salt, cilantro, and chilies.

To make the Uthapa, pour a cup of the batter into an oiled 10-inch skillet, over medium heat. Sprinkle a quarter of the topping mix over, and cook until the Uthapa sets and browns lightly. Turn and cook the other side until the onions are brown. Repeat with the rest of the batter and the topping mix. *Serves 4.*

*D*avid Morris's motivation for opening his bakery typifies an honored tradition in Berkeley: "to make a living doing the thing I most enjoy. . ." Drawing on traditional European recipes, the bakery offers unusual and authentic breads. The Bread Garden has the distinction of being one of the first bakeries in Berkeley to produce what is now a local staple, the handmade baguette. On Sunday mornings long lines form outside his small storefront, as patrons wait patiently to approach the trays of still-warm bread and rolls. Now under new ownership, the Bread Garden offers a vast array of cakes, cookies, and pastries.

Compliments of

BREAD GARDEN
BERKELEY

German Potato Bread

German potato bread is a light-colored, chewy loaf with a dense texture. It is simple to make, muscle-building to knead, and can be ready to eat within three hours.

1 package (1 tablespoon) dry yeast
1½ cups lukewarm water (150° to 115°)
1 cup mashed cooked potatoes, cooled
1 tablespoon vegetable oil
2 teaspoons salt
5 to 6 cups unbleached all-purpose flour
1 egg mixed with
2 tablespoons water
Poppy seeds

Dissolve the yeast in the water in a large bowl for 5 to 10 minutes. Add the potatoes, oil, salt, and 2 cups of the flour. Stir until well blended, then start adding more flour until the dough is quite stiff. Turn the dough out onto a lightly floured surface and knead for 10 minutes, working in more flour until at least 5 cups (but not more than 6) of the flour have been incorporated into the dough. When the kneading is done, the dough should be stiffer than usual bread dough. It will soften while rising. Cover and let rise in a warm place until doubled in size, about 1 hour.

Preheat the oven to 375°. Divide the dough into 2 pieces and shape each like a potato. Place the loaves on a greased baking sheet and cut a 1-inch-deep slit lengthwise down each loaf. Brush the loaf with the egg and water, then liberally dust the loaves with poppy seeds. Place a pan of hot water on the lower rack of the oven, and immediately place the loaves in the oven. Bake for 1 hour, or until no white spots remain on the crust. *Makes 2 loaves.*

NOTE: Unlike most breads, this bread is not allowed to rise again after shaping. This adds to the chewiness of the loaf.

Cinnamon-Swirl Loaves

A fragrant, sweet bread to serve with a fruit salad or to toast as a breakfast bread. This is also a good bread for French toast.

1 package (1 tablespoon) dry yeast
2 cups lukewarm water (105° to 115°)
¾ cup dried instant milk powder
½ cup sugar
7 to 8 cups unbleached all-purpose flour
½ cup oil or melted butter
2 teaspoons salt
2 eggs, lightly beaten
1 egg, mixed with
¼ cup water
¾ cup sugar, mixed with
3 tablespoons ground cinnamon

In a large bowl, dissolve the yeast in the water for 5 to 10 minutes. Stir in the dried milk, sugar, 4 to 5 cups of the flour, oil or melted butter, salt, and 2 beaten eggs. Mix well. Stir in the rest of the flour cup by cup (using as little as possible) until the dough pulls away from the side of the bowl. Turn out onto a lightly floured surface and knead at least 10 minutes, using as little as possible of the remaining flour to keep the dough from sticking. Cover with a clean cloth or plastic wrap and let rise in a warm place until doubled in size, about 1 hour.

After the dough has risen, divide it into 2 equal pieces. Using a rolling pin, roll out each half into a 15-by-7-inch rectangle. Paint each rectangle with the egg-water mixture, then sprinkle each with half of the cinnamon-sugar mixture, leaving 1 inch of one of the short ends of each rectangle uncovered. Roll the rectangles jelly-roll style towards the uncovered edge (the finished rolls will be 7 inches wide) and place each seam side down in an oiled bread pan. Cover the loaves and let rise until doubled, about 1 hour. Brush the tops of the loaves with the remaining egg-water mixture and bake in a preheated 350° oven for 40 minutes. When the loaves are done, they will sound hollow when removed from the pan and tapped on the bottom. *Makes 2 loaves.*

Sticky Buns

The same dough used for Cinnamon-Swirl Loaves can be used to make sticky buns—or you can divide the bread recipe in half to make twelve buns and one loaf of bread.

Dough for Cinnamon-Swirl Loaves, preceding
1 egg, mixed with
¼ cup water
¾ cup sugar, mixed with
3 tablespoons ground cinnamon
1½ cups raisins
½ cup dark brown sugar

After the dough has risen, roll it out into 1 large rectangle 20 inches by 10 inches. Brush the entire rectangle with the egg-water mixture and cover all but a 1-inch edge of the 20-inch side with the cinnamon-sugar mixture. Then sprinkle the raisins generously over the cinnamon-sugar mixture. Roll up the rectangle jelly-roll style towards the uncovered edge and cut into 24 equal pieces.

Oil four 8-inch round cake pans and place the brown sugar evenly over the bottom of each pan. Place 6 pieces of dough in each pan, let rise in a warm place until doubled in size, and bake in a preheated 350° oven for 30 minutes (until tops are nicely browned). Immediately after removing the pans from the oven, run a knife around the edge of the buns, remove from the pans, and invert them on cooling racks. Caution: Be careful not to burn yourself on the hot, runny brown sugar. *Makes 24 sticky buns.*

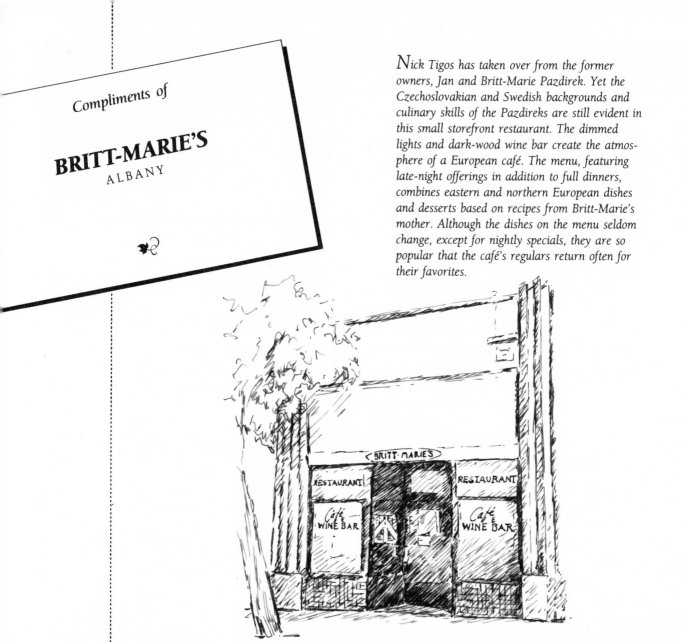

Compliments of

BRITT-MARIE'S
ALBANY

*N*ick Tigos has taken over from the former owners, Jan and Britt-Marie Pazdirek. Yet the Czechoslovakian and Swedish backgrounds and culinary skills of the Pazdireks are still evident in this small storefront restaurant. The dimmed lights and dark-wood wine bar create the atmosphere of a European café. The menu, featuring late-night offerings in addition to full dinners, combines eastern and northern European dishes and desserts based on recipes from Britt-Marie's mother. Although the dishes on the menu seldom change, except for nightly specials, they are so popular that the café's regulars return often for their favorites.

Roasted Peppers with Creamed Feta

This is a simple and delightful appetizer, un-complicated and convenient in that it can be prepared well ahead of serving. If made in larger quantities with several kinds of peppers—red, yellow, green—the plate becomes most colorful.

1 bell pepper (red, yellow, or green)
3 garlic cloves
¼ cup olive oil
½ cup feta cheese
Cilantro leaves to taste

Roast, peel, seed, and julienne the pepper (see Basics). Sauté the garlic cloves in the olive oil until light gold. While still hot, pour the oil and garlic over the pepper strips. In a mixer or food processor, cream the feta with the cilantro leaves. Add a few drops of olive oil if the mixture is too dense. Serve at room temperature with Topinka (following), with the pepper strips arranged around the cheese.
Makes 2 servings.

Topinka

Another simple, satisfying appetizer to serve alone, or with Roasted Peppers with Creamed Feta, preceding.

1 slice rye bread, preferably 1 day old
Olive oil (optional)
1 garlic clove, cut in half, or puréed
   (use a garlic press) and mixed with
   1 teaspoon olive oil
Salt to taste
3 very thin slices Emmenthaler cheese
Hungarian paprika

Sauté the bread in a small amount of olive oil or toast it. While still hot, rub the bread with the garlic clove or spread with garlic-oil purée, sprinkle it with salt, and top with the cheese. Dust with paprika and serve immediately.
Makes 1 serving.

Czech Bread

This peasant bread is even heartier if you use whole-wheat flour rather than white flour. The potato makes for a chewier loaf. This is the bread to use for Topinka, preceding.

2 cups lukewarm water (105° to 115°)
1 package (1 tablespoon) dry yeast
2½ teaspoons salt
1 tablespoon caraway seeds
1 medium-sized potato, cooked, peeled, and grated
2 cups rye flour and 6 cups whole-wheat flour, *or* 8 cups unbleached all-purpose flour, *or* a mixture of white and rye flours totaling 8 cups

Mix the water, yeast, salt, caraway seeds, potato, and 4 cups of the flour in a large bowl. Stir well to blend, incorporating the flour little by little. *Do not knead* at this stage. Place in an oiled bowl and let rise in a warm place for approximately 1 hour, or until the dough is doubled in volume. Punch the dough down and mix in the remaining flour until the dough no longer sticks to the bowl. Turn the dough out onto a lightly floured surface. Knead the dough until all the flour is incorporated, and shape into 2 loaves. Slash the surface of the loaves diagonally with a sharp knife. Let rise in a warm place on a baking sheet that has been oiled or lined with parchment, until bread is doubled, about 1 hour.
   The dough is ready to bake when you gently poke it with your finger and it doesn't spring back. Just before the loaves go into the oven, brush them with tepid water.

Bake in a preheated 450° oven for 15 minutes, or until the loaves are a golden color. Reduce the temperature to 300° and bake for another 45 minutes to 1 hour or until the loaves sound hollow when removed from the pans and tapped on the bottom. Remove the bread from the pans and cool on a rack. *Makes 2 loaves.*

Pear Tart

With the best-quality pears, this is a dessert that can't fail to please. The mock puff pastry makes a splendid shell and is well worth the time and effort involved.

Tart Dough

1¾ cups pastry flour or unbleached all-purpose flour
7 tablespoons cold unsalted butter, cut into small pieces
2 to 3 tablespoons water or heavy cream

Filling

3 juicy ripe pears, about 1 pound
¼ cup sour cream
¼ cup heavy cream
4 tablespoons sugar
2 tablespoons orange liqueur

Whipped unsweetened heavy cream

Sift the flour into a mixing bowl. Add the butter pieces, rubbing them into the flour with your fingertips or cutting them in with 2 knives or a pastry blender. Work the butter in for about a minute, or until the mixture looks like bread crumbs. Add just enough cold water to made the crumbs cohere in a mass. Work the dough with your hands until it is smooth and comes cleanly away from the sides of the bowl. Shape the dough into a ball, wrap in plastic wrap or foil, and refrigerate for at least 15 minutes to allow the dough to relax and the butter to become firm.

On a floured board, roll the dough into a rectangle about ¼ inch thick and 3 times as long as it is wide. Fold over one-third of the length of the rectangle; then fold over the remaining third. Wrap and chill the dough to firm it once more. Roll the dough into a rectangle again and fold as before. Chill again. Repeat rolling and turning once more. After the final turn, refrigerate for at least 1 hour before using. Tightly wrapped dough can safely be kept in the refrigerator for 2 or 3 days, or in the freezer for 2 months. If frozen, defrost it in the refrigerator overnight.

Roll the dough into a circle about ⅛ inch thick. Roll the dough onto the rolling pin, lift it up, and unroll it over a 10-inch tart pan. Press the dough firmly against the bottom and sides of the pan. Roll the pin across the top to cut off the excess dough around the rim. Prick the bottom with a fork. Chill the dough in the tart pan until firm in order to prevent shrinkage. Place aluminum foil filled with un-cooked rice or beans on the bottom of the crust and bake in a preheated 350° oven until the crust is light golden.

Peel, halve, and core the pears. Cut the halves lengthwise into thin slices. Arrange the pear slices in overlapping rows on the prebaked tart shell. Mix the sour cream and heavy cream with the sugar and liqueur. Pour the mixture over the pear slices.

Bake in a preheated 400° oven for 10 to 15 minutes, or until the top is golden. Serve warm or at room temperature, garnished with whipped unsweetened cream. *Makes one 10-inch tart.*

NOTE: The hurried baker can skip the folding of the dough and still create a delicious tart, although the pastry will not be flaky. For a perfectly light and tender pastry: (1) keep the ingredients cold; (2) handle the dough as little and as rapidly as possible.

Compliments of

BROADWAY TERRACE CAFÉ

OAKLAND

Owner Albert Katz supervises and helps to cook a changing menu of astonishing variety and depth. His lighter touch in saucing mesquite-grilled foods has created a special place for the Broadway Terrace among East Bay grill restaurants. It demonstrates the value of professionalism and the importance of the owner's involvement in every aspect of the business. A former restaurant manager and consultant with a degree in business administration, Katz decided to drop out of the large-restaurant business and to apply his remarkable skills to his own personal vision. The result: a small restaurant consisting of several intimate dining areas, tucked away in a wooded residential section of the Oakland hills.

Gorgonzola-Pear Salad

*O*ne of the most delicious salads around, this is a good way to begin or end any meal. Use a Gorgonzola that is crumbly rather than creamy, or your favorite blue cheese. It is also possible to substitute a sweet vinegar such as balsamic or another well-aged, mellow vinegar. Walnut oil is available from gourmet grocers.

The quality of the pears is crucial to this salad. They should be ripe, sweet, and creamy in texture—never mushy.

1 head romaine lettuce
¾ cup whole walnuts

Walnut Oil Vinaigrette

¼ cup reserved toasted walnuts
½ garlic clove
1 tablespoon red wine vinegar and
  1 tablespoon raspberry vinegar,
  or 2 tablespoons balsamic vinegar
Salt and pepper
3 tablespoons walnut oil
3 tablespoons light vegetable oil

½ cup crumbled Gorgonzola (domestic Tolibia
  if possible)
2 pears (red D'Anjou if possible), cored and
  cut lengthwise in eighths
½ bunch watercress

Separate the lettuce leaves, discarding the outer ones. Toast the walnuts in a preheated 325° oven for 5 minutes. Prepare a vinaigrette by puréeing ¼ cup of the toasted walnuts and the garlic. Add the vinegars and salt and pep-

per. While slowly stirring, add the oils to emulsify.

Lay out the whole romaine leaves in a bowl and toss with the remaining ½ cup toasted walnuts, ½ cup of vinaigrette, and Gorgonzola and set on 4 serving plates. Top with pear slices and watercress and add any Gorgonzola left in the mixing bowl. *Serves 4.*

Fresh Corn Timbale
with Red Pepper Vinaigrette

*W*e made this recipe twice during the testing just because we liked it so much. This type of recipe is characteristic of the Berkeley-area style of cooking in that it is a classic concept adapted to local ingredients and taste, with the addition of something unique—in this case a vinaigrette based on roasted red peppers (which could also be used for salads or on grilled fish).

2 ears corn
⅓ cup heavy cream
⅔ cup half and half
1 teaspoon sugar
2 eggs
1 egg yolk
Salt and ground white pepper to taste
Red Pepper Vinaigrette, following

Steam the corn for 5 minutes or until tender. Scrape the kernels off and put into a blender or food processor with the heavy cream. Purée until smooth.

Heat the half and half in a pan with the sugar until just scalded. Remove from the heat and add the puréed corn; let steep for a few minutes.

Beat the eggs and yolk together in a mixing bowl. Put the corn-cream mixture into a sieve and strain into the bowl, pressing with a rubber spatula to extract the juices, or use a food mill. Add the salt and white pepper.

Butter six 3-ounce timbale molds, fill, and place them in a roasting pan. Pour boiling water into the pan to halfway up the molds. Bake in a preheated 375° oven for 20 to 25 minutes, or until firm, lightly browned on top, and slightly puffed. Unmold onto a plate and surround with Red Pepper Vinaigrette. *Serves 6.*

Red Pepper Vinaigrette

3 large red bell peppers
1 teaspoon chopped shallot
¼ teaspoon chopped garlic
1 tablespoon Dijon mustard
⅓ cup champagne vinegar or white wine
    vinegar*
¼ teaspoon salt
Pinch of ground white pepper and cayenne
¾ cup plus 2 tablespoons good olive oil

Roast, peel, seed, and chop the peppers (see Basics). In a blender or food processor, combine the shallot, garlic, mustard, vinegar, salt, white pepper, and cayenne. Slowly add the olive oil until the mixture thickens. With the machine running, add the roasted peppers. Taste and adjust seasonings. *Serves 6.*

*Use 5 percent acidity vinegar. Some champagne vinegars are 7 percent and too tart.

Four Sauces for Grilled Fish

These sauces are for simply cooked fish: grilled, poached or sautéed. In the best of the developing tradition of California cooking, these gems are straightforward, rely on seasonal components, and manage to unite seemingly disparate elements. Each sauce recipe is followed by a recommendation for the fish it should accompany, but don't be shy about combining any of the sauces with the best fish you can find at the time. You might even want to try some of them with a simply cooked meat.

Orange-Thyme Butter

1½ cups fresh orange juice
½ teaspoon chopped shallot
1 cup (2 sticks) unsalted butter, softened
1 tablespoon minced fresh thyme
¼ teaspoon distilled vinegar
Salt

In a sauté pan or skillet, boil the orange juice and chopped shallot over medium-high heat until reduced to a syrupy consistency (about 3 tablespoons of the sauce will remain).

In a bowl with a wooden spoon or in a blender or food processor, cream the butter. Add the orange syrup, thyme, and vinegar and blend until well incorporated. Add salt to taste. Serve a dollop of butter on each piece of fish. Redfish, salmon, and sea basses are recommended. *Serves 6.*

Fennel-Citrus Relish

1 large fennel bulb
½ cup unsalted butter
1 orange
1 lemon
½ pink grapefruit
Salt

Cut the fennel bulb in half lengthwise. Slice the white bulb and 1 inch of the green stems into long, thin slices. In a large sauté pan or skillet, cook the fennel and ¼ cup of the butter over medium heat until the fennel is soft but still crunchy, about 5 minutes.

Peel the citrus fruits, scraping away as much white pith as possible. Break into segments and cut into bite-sized pieces. Add the citrus to the fennel in the pan and warm gently. Stir the remaining ¼ cup of the butter into the fennel mixture, being very careful not to break apart the citrus pieces. Add salt to taste. Serve alongside fish. Recommended: sole, fluke, halibut. *Serves 6.*

Grape-Ginger Glaze

The amount of honey used in this recipe should balance the acid in the grapes. If the grapes are very sweet, you might want to omit the honey.

1 pound red or purple seedless grapes
1 tablespoon red wine vinegar
1 tablespoon honey
1 cup dry red wine
½ cup thinly sliced fresh ginger

Save a few grapes for garnish and place the rest in a large sauté pan or skillet with the vinegar, honey, wine, and ginger. Bring to a boil, reduce heat and simmer for 5 minutes or until most of the liquid is gone.

In a blender or food processor, purée the grape mixture for 1 minute. Force through a fine sieve back into the sauté pan. Return to medium heat and boil the juice down until it forms a syrupy consistency. Brush onto the fish and garnish with the reserved grapes. Serve on shark, yellow-tailed jack, or tuna. *Serves 6.*

Raspberry and Rosemary Vinaigrette

¼ cup raspberry vinegar
1 teaspoon Dijon mustard
1 tablespoon chopped fresh rosemary
1 teaspoon chopped shallot
Dash salt and ground white pepper
24 fresh raspberries
1 cup olive oil

In a blender or food processor, combine the vinegar, mustard, rosemary, shallot, salt, pepper, and most of the raspberries (save a few to use as garnish). Purée until smooth. Then, with the motor running, add the oil slowly. Taste the vinaigrette and, if it lacks sweetness, add a dash of sugar. Serve with swordfish, marlin, tuna, or other oily fish. *Serves 6.*

Brie Cheesecake

This dessert is rich without being heavy. The use of soft-ripening double or triple cream cheese gives cheesecake a whole new personality. The recipe is simple; just be sure to cream the cheese with the sugar before adding the eggs, and scrape the sides and bottom of the bowl several times during the mixing process. Fresh fruit sauce or purée would be especially good with this cake.

10 ounces natural cream cheese
12 ounces skinned Brie cheese, or a mixture
   of Brie and another French triple *crème*
   cheese
1¼ cups sugar
5 eggs

In a blender or food processor, blend the cream cheese, Brie, and ¾ cup of the sugar until smooth. Stop the machine and scrape down the sides once or twice while blending. Beat the eggs lightly; add them and the remaining ½ cup of the sugar to the cheese-sugar mixture. Purée until smooth and liquid.

Pour into a well-buttered 9-inch spring-form pan. Set the pan in a larger container filled with boiling water. The water bath should come halfway up the sides of the spring-form pan.

Place in a preheated 325° oven and bake for 1¼ hours, or until lightly browned and firm to the touch. Remove the cake from the water bath and cool. Invert onto a plate, remove the bottom of the spring-form pan, and smooth out the surface of the cheesecake. Top with a fresh fruit sauce or purée, depending on seasonal availability. *Serves 8 to 10.*

When Alice Waters was asked why she designed a tiny Italian-style stand-up café, she replied, "I wanted a little place to go for breakfast." Fanny's breakfast menu offers seasonal juices, fresh muffins, café au lait served in bowls, and blue Aracuna eggs prepared in a number of styles. Pizzas, lovely Provençal-style light sandwiches, and delectable desserts are served for lunch. Café Fanny has recently expanded its horizons to include catering and baked goods available outside the Café, at select retail shops and restaurants. Good things do come in small packages!

Compliments of

CAFÉ FANNY
BERKELEY

Rooted in the cuisine of southern France, and so simple as to be utterly at the mercy of the quality of the ingredients, the recipes that follow are classics in the sandwich genre, and very much in the Chez Panisse tradition.

Grilled Mozzarella and Tapenade Sandwich

Tapenade

2 cups Niçoise olives, pitted and chopped
3 tablespoons capers, rinsed and squeezed
2 cloves garlic, chopped
1 or 2 anchovy fillets
½ cup olive oil
Juice of ¼ lemon

Sandwich

1 pound fresh, creamy, sweet mozzarella
  cheese
1 loaf white, dense bread

To make the Tapenade, chop by hand the olives, capers, garlic, and anchovies and mix together. Add the olive oil and the lemon.

For each sandwich, spread 1 slice of bread with 1½ tablespoons of tapenade. Top with 2 thin slices of mozzarella and a second slice of bread. Brush both sides with olive oil. Grill until cheese is melted and the outside is golden brown. *Makes 10 sandwiches.*

Roasted Tomato Sandwich

12 ripe garden tomatoes
2 tablespoons olive oil
Salt and pepper
1 loaf sour-dough baguette
6 medium shallots, minced
2 tablespoons Balsamic vinegar
1 bunch opal basil leaves

Wash and core the tomatoes, and slice in half. Place flat-side-up on a cookie sheet. Brush with olive oil and sprinkle with lots of salt and pepper. Roast until soft, about 10 to 20 minutes in a 350° oven. Peel the skin and cut each half into pieces about ½-inch long.

Cut the bread into ¼-inch slices, toast them, and brush with olive oil. Mash the diced shallots and vinegar together in a small bowl and then spread this mixture on the bread. Place the tomatoes on the toast slices and garnish with opal basil. *Serves 12.*

Chicken Salad Sandwich

1 pound chicken breasts
¼ cup pitted Calamata or Niçoise olives
⅛ cup rinsed capers
⅛ cup diced red onions
⅓ cup cornichons, finely sliced crosswise
⅓ cup diced red peppers
¾ cup diced celery
1 loaf sourdough bread or 12 squares Italian
   fougasse or 1 sourdough baguette
1 cup mayonnaise, following

Mayonnaise

1 whole egg
3 egg yolks
1½ teaspoons mustard
1 cup olive oil
2½ cups peanut oil
2 tablespoons lemon juice
2 tablespoons champagne vinegar
1¼ teaspoons salt
Cracked white pepper, to taste

Make the Mayonnaise first. Mix together the whole egg, egg yolks, and mustard. Combine the olive and peanut oils, add slowly to the emulsified eggs and season with lemon juice, vinegar, salt, and white pepper.

Roast the chicken breasts and shred into ½-inch pieces. Pit and roughly chop the olives, and mix with the capers, onions, cornichons, peppers, and celery. Mix in the mayonnaise, adding more or less according to taste.

Spread on sliced sourdough toast or on Italian fougasse squares. *Makes 8 sandwiches.*

Compliments of

CAFÉ GLENDA
BERKELEY

Berkeley abounds with wonderful ethnic restaurants and Café Glenda, at the top of Solano Avenue, adds Filipino cuisine to the variety available. Filipino cooking blends Malaysian, Chinese, and Spanish influences. The restaurant specializes in grilled dishes and stews. Glenda Barretto, one of the owners, also operates restaurants in Manila.

Garlic Chicken Paillards

Grilling over natural wood charcoal is a basic technique of Filipino cuisine. This dish adds California herbs to that tradition. Simple grilled vegetables and Filipino Garlic Rice make a complete meal.

Marinade

Juice of 1 lemon
½ teaspoon minced garlic
½ teaspoon minced fresh basil
½ teaspoon minced fresh oregano
Salt and pepper to taste
¼ cup olive oil

4 boneless chicken breast fillets, lightly
   flattened

Combine the lemon juice, garlic, herbs, and salt and pepper with the olive oil. Marinate the chicken for 2 hours, then grill over charcoal until just done. Serve with Garlic Rice, following. *Serves 2.*

Garlic Rice

2 cups steamed rice
¼ teaspoon minced garlic
Salt to taste
Banana leaves, corn husks, or aluminum foil

Mix the rice, garlic, and salt. Roll up in leaves, husks, or foil and grill along with the chicken. *Serves 2.*

Lumpia

This is a recipe of forbidding length, but it is not very complicated. Lumpia may be served as a first course or as a hot main dish salad. The vegetables are sautéed al dente, rolled in a delicate thin crêpe, then enlivened with a garlic and lemon grass sauce. There is really nothing like making your own wrappers, and these are wonderfully fresh and tender. The wrappers and sauce can be made earlier in the day; only the filling needs to be done at the last minute.

Wrappers

1 egg
1 cup flour
1 cup cornstarch
2½ cups water

Filling

½ teaspoon minced garlic
2 tablespoons vegetable oil
1 small onion, julienned
1 whole boneless breast of chicken or 2 boneless legs or thighs, cut into thin strips
1 cup chicken stock
1 teaspoon sugar
1 teaspoon salt
¼ teaspoon white pepper
2 small carrots, julienned
1 small jicama, julienned
¼ pound green beans, julienned
1 cup shredded cabbage
Greenleaf lettuce
¼ cup chopped unsalted peanuts

Sauce

⅓ cup brown sugar
1 stalk lemon grass, roughly chopped
1 teaspoon minced garlic
⅓ cup Chinese or Filipino soy sauce
2 cups water
1 tablespoon cornstarch dissolved in 3 tablespoons water

Make the wrappers first. Whisk all ingredients in a medium bowl until smooth. Strain and whisk again.

Over low heat, heat an 8-inch nonstick skillet. Off the heat pour just enough of the batter, about 3 tablespoons, to cover the surface of the pan, making sure that the mixture is spread thinly and evenly. Return the skillet to the heat until the crêpe sets. Do not brown. Remove from the heat and invert the skillet over a flat surface. The crêpe should fall out. Allow to cool and set aside. Repeat this procedure for each crêpe. *Makes about 12 crêpes.*

For the sauce, combine the sugar, lemon grass, garlic, and soy sauce with the water and bring to a simmer. Cook for 5 minutes, stirring occasionally. Add the dissolved cornstarch and simmer until the sauce is thickened and clear. Strain out the chunks of lemon grass and set aside. This sauce can be refrigerated for days and reheated when needed. *Makes about 2 cups.*

In a medium wok or sauté pan, brown the garlic in the oil, then add the onion and chicken and cook until they are half done. Add the chicken stock, sugar, and salt and pepper. Bring to a boil and add the carrots, jicama, and beans. When the beans and carrots are *al dente*, add the cabbage and cook until it is just wilted.

To assemble the Lumpia, wrap the hot filling in a crêpe with a small piece of lettuce. Pour a small amount of sauce over the Lumpia and garnish with chopped peanuts. Serve the remaining sauce on the side. *Serves 4 to 6.*

"We work to create food to be experienced in a thoughtful way with the eyes, palate, and mind." This is the way Hi-Sak Dong, the restaurant manager (and architect) and Sanjo Dong, the chef (and visual artist) characterize their approach to their restaurant. The food reflects Asian, French, and Californian influences, with a strong emphasis on artistic presentation. The striking dining room is decorated with paintings by Sanjo and other local artists and most of the staff have some background in the arts.

Compliments of

CAFÉ PASTORAL
BERKELEY

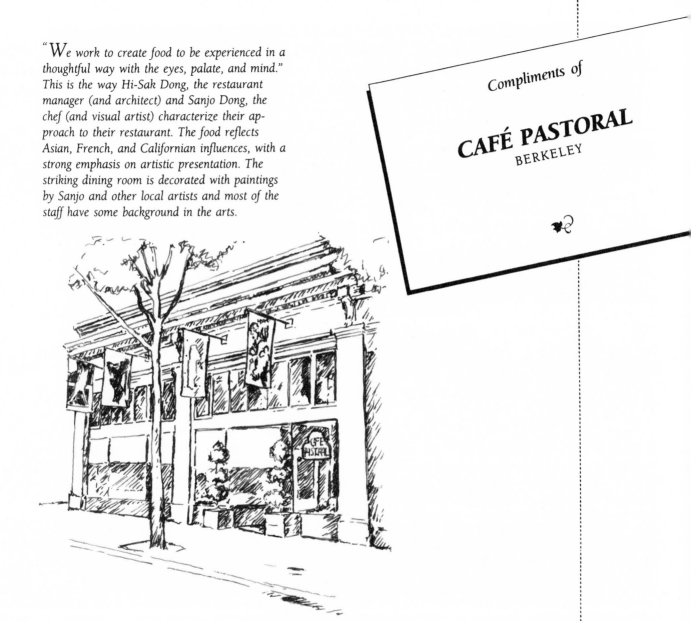

Artichoke and Leek Soup

This unusual soup is rich and flavorful.

½ cup onions, cut in medium dice
½ cup celery, cut in medium dice
½ cup carrots, peeled and cut in medium dice
4 tablespoons (½ stick) butter
2 cups leeks, chopped, white part only*
1 to 1½ quarts chicken stock
2 russet potatoes, peeled and sliced
5 cloves garlic
5 or 6 fresh artichokes, or 1 package frozen
  artichoke hearts
¼ cup fresh lemon juice plus extra for
  seasoning
1 cup heavy cream
Salt
Pepper
Crème fraîche or sour cream for garnish

In a large, heavy nonreactive saucepan, gently sauté the onions, celery, and carrots in the butter until tender. Add the leeks. Cook, covered, until tender.

Add the stock, potatoes, and garlic and bring to a boil. Reduce to a simmer over medium heat and cook until the potatoes are done.

Meanwhile, prepare the artichokes. With a large, sharp chef's knife, cut off the stem and the top 1½ inches of the leaves. Break off the outer leaves until the remaining leaves are mostly yellow. Trim off the dark green from the base of the heart, quarter the artichoke, and trim out the choke and the inner purple leaves. Reserve the hearts in a quart of water to which has been added ¼ cup lemon juice to prevent discoloration.

When the potatoes are done, add the artichokes and cook, covered, over medium heat until tender, about 20 to 30 minutes, stirring occasionally to prevent sticking. Purée the soup and then pass it through a sieve to remove the fibers. (This is tedious but essential.)

Return the soup to a clean pot, add the cream, and heat, adjusting the thickness by adding more stock or cream, or by reducing. (Beware of sticking if reducing.) Adjust the seasoning with salt, pepper, and lemon juice. The acidity of the lemon juice is important for balancing the richness of the cream. Garnish with dollops of crème fraîche or sour cream. *Serves 6.*

*To clean leeks well, cut the green part off, quarter them lengthwise, then chop into 1-inch lengths, separating the layers into a pot of cold water. Soak, rinse, then soak and rinse again in clean water. All grit must be removed.

Dry-Aged New York Steak with Roquefort Cheese Sauce

Dry aging is a process that can only be done with the full cut of beef, i.e., with the whole New York, or top sirloin, or rib, preferably with the bone attached. The meat is hung so that air can circulate around it freely on all sides for about two weeks, during which time it loses a lot of moisture and turns an absolutely ugly dark brown on the outside. It is then trimmed and cut to reveal the still-red meat inside. The flavors and fats of the meat are concentrated, resulting in a more tender, flavorful, and expensive steak. It is perfectly acceptable to use conventionally aged beef for this simple and unusually good recipe.

Salt and pepper
Flour
One 10-ounce dry-aged New York steak
1½ to 2 tablespoons clarified butter
½ teaspoon shallots, chopped
1 tablespoon cognac or white wine
2 ounces crumbled Roquefort cheese
½ tablespoon Dijon mustard
3 tablespoons butter

Salt, pepper, and flour the steak lightly on both sides. In a preheated skillet over medium heat, sauté the steak in the clarified butter for about 2 minutes per side, or to taste. Remove the steak and, if the cooking butter is burned, pour it out. Deglaze the pan with the cognac or wine and, when the alcohol has burned off, add the shallots, cheese, and mustard, allowing the cheese to melt completely. If a milder Roquefort flavor is desired, the sauce may be attenuated with a bit of cream. Whisk in the butter and drape the steak with the sauce. *Serves 1.*

Axonometric Appetizer

In architecture an axonometric projection is a rendition of a structure that allows one to view into and see the layers of the structure. With this recipe, you end up with a multistoried tower of wonton skins, smoked salmon, and raw tuna, garnished as artfully as you like with snow peas, daikon, chervil, and chives.

½ cup clarified butter
30 wonton skins
Half a daikon root
24 to 36 snow peas
½ pound tuna, sliced as if for *sashimi*, approximately ⅛-inch thick
½ pound smoked salmon, sliced
Chervil
Chives
Nori-maki (seaweed sheets), cut into 1-inch by 3-inch pieces

Dressing

¼ cup sherry vinegar
1 tablespoon *wasabi* (Japanese horseradish)
2 tablespoons soy sauce
½ cup olive oil

For the dressing, mix the vinegar, wasabi, and soy sauce well, then whisk in the olive oil and set aside.

Bring the clarified butter to medium heat. Fry the wonton skins until they are golden brown on both sides. Remove and drain on paper towels.

Julienne the daikon into long strips. Remove the strings from the snow peas and blanch them in salted water for 35 seconds.

To assemble the appetizer, lay the daikon strips on 6 individual plates, put the fried wonton skins on the daikon, then alternate 2 layers of tuna and smoked salmon with a single layer of wonton skins separating the layers of fish. You should end up with a standing cylindrical tower of layers of wonton skins and fresh and smoked fish. Garnish the plates with the snow peas, chervil, chives, and nori, then ladle the dressing lightly over the towers. *Serves 6.*

*C*ollectively owned and operated, the Cheese Board is located at the heart of North Berkeley's "gourmet ghetto." Customers are greeted by an inviting wood and glass counter, running the depth of the store, which displays every cheese you could ever imagine, and many more beyond that. Is all this variety confusing? The people behind the counter will be delighted to offer you suggestions and a taste of anything you'd like to try. Your selections will then be cut to your specifications, weighed, wrapped, and packaged in recycled paper bags, an unusual policy even in ecology-minded Berkeley. In addition to the cheeses, the shop offers magnificent home-baked breads, fresh dairy products, and pizza slices for a gourmet lunch on the run. Two doors south, the new Cheese Board Annex offers its rustic pizza breads, and pre-cut cheeses.

Compliments of

CHEESE BOARD
BERKELEY

Asiago Bread

Created by Bob Waks, this is a splendid, easy bread, fragrant with onions, cheese, and herbs. It can be made with different cheeses and herbs, but this particular combination is especially successful. Asiago bread makes wonderful toast.

1 package (1 tablespoon) dry yeast
2 cups lukewarm water (105° to 115°)
6 cups unbleached all-purpose flour
2 cups chopped onions
2 teaspoons dried marjoram
2 teaspoons salt
2 cups domestic Asiago cheese, cut in small
  cubes (about 12 ounces)
Sesame seeds

Dissolve the yeast in the water in a large bowl; let sit until foaming, 5 to 15 minutes. Mix all the other ingredients, except the cheese and sesame seeds, into the bowl, adding enough flour to make a medium-stiff dough. Gather the dough into a ball and knead on a lightly floured surface for 10 minutes. Cover with a damp towel and let rise in a warm place for 1 hour or until the dough doubles in size. Incorporate the cheese into the dough.

Divide the dough into 6 strands and braid them into 2 loaves. Brush or spray the loaves with water and sprinkle liberally with sesame seeds. Place immediately in a preheated 400° oven for 10 minutes. Reduce the heat to 350° and bake for 30 to 45 minutes, or until the loaves are well browned and sound hollow when removed from the pans and tapped on the bottom. *Makes 2 loaves.*

Mock Boursin

Herbed Cream Cheese

This cheese is simple to make. The recipe allows you to modify the seasonings if you wish, and it will produce a quantity sufficient to meet your guests' demands. Be sure to use natural cream cheese without emulsifiers, or you won't be able to reproduce the light texture that is essential to this spread. And use only fresh chives and parsley.

1 to 2 garlic cloves
½ cup minced chives
½ cup minced parsley
⅔ pound natural cream cheese, at room
  temperature
⅔ cup baker's cheese
Salt to taste

Crush the garlic, chives, and parsley in a mortar, then blend into the cheese with a wooden spoon. Add salt to taste. *Makes 2 cups.*

In the best tradition of a French three-star restaurant, owner Alice Waters has developed a network of purveyors who supply her restaurant with products ranging from baby lettuces and fresh herbs to the flowers for the arrangements that are a hallmark of Chez Panisse. Waters popularized the concept of a menu that changes daily and uses seasonal ingredients in surprising combinations. The results are exotic and intriguing, and Chez Panisse has developed an international reputation. The restaurant has always been the proving ground for new dishes, as well as the training ground for a corps of chefs, many of whom have gone on to start their own restaurants.

Located in an unassuming, Craftsman-style building, Chez Panisse has two dining areas: the downstairs, serving one menu each evening, is more formal, while the Café upstairs is casual and bustling and offers a broader, less-expensive menu.

Compliments of

CHEZ PANISSE
BERKELEY

Grilled Summer Vegetable Pasta

Arrange your meal preparations so that there will be no distractions when grilling the vegetables for this dish, as they scorch easily, particularly the eggplant and onions. Roma, or plum, tomatoes work best for this dish; other tomatoes are too juicy. Consider grilling the vegetables an hour before serving; they will hold up well. If you do grill the vegetables ahead of time and cook the tomato-garlic element of the sauce in advance, the dish can be completed in five minutes.

2 salt-packed anchovies
Virgin olive oil
3 peppers: yellow, green, or red
6 to 8 small Japanese eggplants
Salt and pepper to taste
8 Roma (plum) tomatoes
1 young red onion
1 to 2 garlic cloves
A few basil leaves
Fresh *tagliatelle* pasta for 2 (6 ounces)
Freshly ground black pepper

Fillet and rinse the anchovies. Pound them in a mortar with a little olive oil to make a smooth paste.

Light a mesquite charcoal fire in an open grill. While the charcoal is still flaming, grill the peppers so that the skin is black and blistered all around. Peel and seed the peppers (see Basics), then cut them into wide strips. Cut the unpeeled eggplants in lengthwise slices about ¼ inch thick. Brush the slices with olive oil and season with salt and pepper. Grill them over the hot fire a few minutes on each side so that they are lightly browned. Cut the tomatoes in half and season with salt and pepper. Grill them skin side down until they get a little color and begin to soften. Slice the onion in rings. Brush with olive oil, season, and grill until browned and tender. Mince the garlic. Cut the basil leaves into a chiffonnade.

Combine the anchovy paste, tomato halves, garlic, and a tablespoon of olive oil in a sauté pan or skillet. Cook gently for a few minutes until the tomatoes release their juices and form a sauce. Add the grilled vegetables and continue to simmer a few minutes more.

Cook the pasta in a large amount of boiling salted water about 2 to 3 minutes until *al dente*; drain and add to the vegetables. Season with black pepper and toss the noodles well in the juices. Serve garnished with all the vegetables and the chiffonnade of basil.
Serves 2.

Almond Semifreddo

Elegant and spectacular, this dessert exacts a price in effort. A sponge cake (made to rise only by the air beaten into a mixture of eggs and sugar, into which is folded flour and butter) is baked and soaked in kirsch. Then praline (yes, you make it), chocolate, and whipped cream are folded into a tricky custard, cooked by the heat of a syrup that must be at a specific temperature, to make an ice cream. The cake and ice cream are frozen together, then unmolded and decorated with fine pipings of chocolate. Your guests will be astounded! And so will you, for following the recipe exactly does yield successful results. And there is the advantage that the dessert can, and even should, be made the day ahead. Since this recipe makes two semifreddos, one can be frozen to serve later. Two semifreddos will serve ten to twelve people, making this an excellent dessert for a large party. Finally, match the labor investment with a material one; buy a bottle of imported kirsch. It has the real flavor, and no domestic imitation can match it.

Cake

3 eggs
½ cup sugar
⅔ cup cake flour
⅛ teaspoon salt
2 tablespoons warm melted butter
½ teaspoon vanilla extract

Praline

¼ cup sugar
1 tablespoon water
¼ cup unblanched whole almonds

3 tablespoons kirsch mixed with
3 tablespoons water

Filling

¼ cup sugar
4 tablespoons water
3 egg yolks
1 cup heavy cream
1½ tablespoons kirsch
1 ounce (1 square) finely chopped semisweet chocolate
Semisweet chocolate

Make the cake first. Butter a 9-inch-square cake pan, lining the bottom with parchment or waxed paper. Put the eggs and sugar in a stainless-steel mixing bowl. Sift the cake flour onto a piece of waxed paper, then measure it into a bowl, then mix in the salt.

Beat the eggs and sugar together over hot water until they are warm to the touch. Remove the mixture from the heat and beat until it is thick and almost white. The bubbles in the mixture should be very fine, and it should hold a shape for 2 or 3 seconds when the beater is lifted from it.

Put the flour into a sieve and begin to shake a thin layer of flour over the egg mixture. Fold it in, giving the spatula a shake as you bring it up through the flour to break up any lumps that might form. Do not fold the flour in completely. Shake in some more flour and continue in this way until all the flour is almost, but not quite completely, folded in.

Check the butter to be sure it feels slightly warm to the touch, and put the vanilla in it. Dribble some of it very lightly over the top of the batter; don't let it sink through. Fold it carefully with a few strokes and finish adding the rest of the butter in the same way. Be very careful not to overwork the batter or it will deflate. The batter should take about 3 additions altogether.

Pour into the prepared pan and bake in a preheated 350° oven for about 25 minutes, or until the top springs back when it is pressed lightly and the cake is beginning to pull away from the sides of the pan. Cool in the pan 5 minutes; then turn out on a rack to finish cooling.

Make the praline next. Butter a 9-inch pan. Heat the sugar and water in a small, heavy, light-colored saucepan. (It's hard to keep track of the color of cooking sugar in a dark pan.) When the sugar has melted, add the almonds and continue cooking, stirring slightly when necessary, until the sugar has turned a light caramel color. If sugar begins to crystallize on the almonds, stir them around gently until the sugar melts off them. When all the sugar is melted and caramelized, pour it into the buttered pan, making sure the nuts are in a single layer. Cool, turn out, and chop fine by hand.

Line two 9-by-5-inch loaf pans with plastic wrap and cut a piece of the cake to fit the bottom of each. Sprinkle the cake with the kirsch-water mixture.

To make the filling, put the sugar and water into a small saucepan and cook to 230°, or until it spins a 1-inch thread when a spoon is dipped in and pulled out. While that cooks, beat the egg yolks until they hold a shape. When the syrup is ready, pour it into the egg yolks in a thin stream, being careful to beat

constantly and to beat where the syrup is hitting the yolks so they don't curdle. Beat over ice until cool and thick enough to hold a shape.

Whip the cream with the kirsch until it is as thick as the egg mixture. Fold them together. (The resulting mixture must be thick enough to hold the praline and chocolate in suspension.)

Fold in the chocolate and the praline and pour into the pans on top of the cake. Cover with plastic wrap and freeze.

To serve, cut in slices about ¾ inch thick. Melt a little chocolate and put through a very fine pastry tube in slanting lines across each slice (or use the tines of a fork). *Serves 10 to 12 (makes 2 semifreddos).*

NOTE: A hazelnut variation can be made by substituting ¼ cup hazelnuts for the almonds. Toast them in a 375° oven for 5 minutes, then cool them and rub off as many of their skins as possible. Proceed, substituting cognac for the kirsch in the recipe above.

Macadamia Nut and Coconut Tart

Exotic ingredients and old-fashioned techniques combine to make an unusually good dessert.

Pastry Shell

½ cup unsalted butter
1 cup unbleached all-purpose flour
1 tablespoon sugar
3 to 4 drops each almond and vanilla extract
1 tablespoon water

½ cup unsweetened shredded coconut
1¼ cups macadamia nuts
6 tablespoons butter
3 tablespoons honey
3 tablespoons heavy cream
3 egg yolks
⅜ cup brown sugar
Vanilla extract to taste

To make the tart shell, cut the butter into bits and let it soften slightly. Mix the flour with the sugar in a bowl. With a pastry cutter or with your fingers, cut the butter into the flour mixture until it resembles very coarse meal. Mix the almond and vanilla extracts with the water and quickly stir into the butter and flour. Gather the dough into a ball and flatten it slightly. Cover it with plastic wrap and chill for at least 1 hour.

Allow the dough to stand at room temperature until it is malleable, then press it into a 9-inch tart ring. (Do not use a black tart pan or the shell will burn when you prebake it.) Cover the shell lightly with plastic wrap and chill for an hour in the freezer.

Bake the tart shell in the lower third of a preheated 375° oven for about 25 minutes, or until it is golden brown. Prick the bottom gently during the baking as it begins to puff. Remove the shell from the oven, cool, and set aside.

Toast the coconut and nuts in the preheated 375° oven until light golden brown, stirring occasionally to toast it evenly—it will take 2 or 3 minutes. Toast the nuts at the same time until lightly browned.

Melt the butter with the honey, stir in the cream, and stir that combination into the egg yolks and sugar, whisking just until thoroughly mixed. When the nuts have cooled enough to handle, chop them coarsely (into ¼-inch to ⅜-inch chunks) and shake them in a strainer to remove the dusty particles.

Add the nuts and coconut to the sugar mixture, stirring to mix, and add a little vanilla to taste. Pour into the prebaked shell and bake in a preheated 375° oven for about 20 minutes or until set. Serve with blood orange or tangerine ice cream or *crème Chantilly. Serves 8.*

Compliments of

CHRISTOPHER'S CAFÉ
BERKELEY

Trained in top restaurants, Christopher Cheung is a good example of a "new" Berkeley chef. He has synthesized a mixed (Asian/Mexican) culinary background to produce wonderfully innovative and eclectic fare. Indeed, his restaurant has become so popular that he has moved from his original cramped quarters to a larger location. He explains his approach: "I combine Chinese frying techniques and fresh Mexican and Thai chilies to create interesting and spicy recipes."

Recently, Christopher's Nothing Fancy Cafe opened on San Pablo Avenue, serving sophisticated Mexican and Southwestern lunch items, along with some of the best hamburgers in Berkeley.

Risotto with Smoked Poussin, Saffron, Chanterelles, and Golden Tomatoes

This wonderful risotto calls for some hard-to-find ingredients that are worth the search. If you are unable to find them, substitute your choice of smoked meat for the poussin (chicken or turkey are good choices), good vine-ripened red tomatoes for the golden tomatoes, and a mixture of fresh domestic and dried wild mushrooms for the chanterelles. See the Pasta Shop's recipe, page 142, for preparation technique.

1 smoked poussin, boned and cut into small dice (about 10 ounces meat)
6 to 7 cups chicken stock
1 cup golden tomatoes
2 red bell peppers (if using red tomatoes, use one red bell pepper and one golden bell pepper)
1 cup chanterelle mushrooms, diced
¼ cup light olive oil
1 garlic clove, minced
½ cup dry white wine
Pinch saffron
2 tablespoons minced fresh oregano
1 small yellow onion, minced
2 tablespoons clarified butter
2 tablespoons light olive oil
1 pound Italian Arborio rice
2 bay leaves
½ cup unsalted butter
¾ cup freshly grated Parmesan (or use half Parmesan and half Romano)
Salt and pepper
Chopped fresh parsley

Put the bones from the poussin into a large saucepan with the chicken stock and allow it to simmer while you prepare the rest of the ingredients. Roast the tomatoes under a broiler until they are soft and the skins are browned; dice. Roast, peel, and seed the peppers (see Basics); dice.

In a sauté pan or skillet, sauté the chanterelles in the olive oil until lightly browned. Add the tomatoes, peppers, garlic, white wine, saffron, oregano, smoked poussin, and 2 cups of the stock (reserve the remainder of the stock for risotto). Simmer for a few minutes and set the mixture aside.

In a large saucepan, sauté the onion gently in the butter and olive oil until it is soft and translucent, but not colored. Add the rice and cook another few minutes, stirring to coat each grain of rice with oil. Add the bay leaves and 1 cup of simmering stock and stir until it is absorbed. Add another cup of stock and continue in this fashion until the rice is done, but still chewy, keeping the liquid level such that the risotto is creamy. Avoid overcooking. Add the reserved chanterelle-poussin mixture and cook for another few minutes. Remove the bay leaves and stir in the butter and ⅓ cup of the Parmesan cheese. Season with salt and pepper to taste and garnish with remaining Parmesan and chopped parsley. *Serves 6 to 8.*

Green Chicken Stew with Lemon Grass, Jalapeños, and Lime

Subtly flavored, just short of scorchingly hot, this stew is an intriguing blend of flavors.

Marinade

1 teaspoon minced fresh ginger
½ teaspoon minced garlic
2 tablespoons peanut oil

1 whole chicken breast, skinned, boned, and
  halved
2½ cups chicken stock
2 lemon grass stalks
1 teaspoon minced fresh ginger
½ teaspoon minced garlic
1 bunch cilantro, roughly chopped
  (about ¼ cup chopped cilantro)
4 green lettuce leaves, roughly chopped
2 *jalapeño* chilies, seeded and roughly
  chopped
1 teaspoon oyster sauce
½ teaspoon sugar
½ teaspoon ground fennel seeds
Peanut oil
Additional chicken stock as needed
Salt

Combine the marinade ingredients and rub into the chicken. Marinate for 30 minutes. Simmer the chicken stock with lemon grass for 30 minutes while the chicken marinates. In a food processor or blender, purée the ginger and garlic, cilantro, lettuce, jalapeños, oyster sauce, sugar, and ground fennel with 1 cup of the chicken stock.

Sauté the marinated chicken breasts in peanut oil until browned on both sides. Remove and cut into chunks. Place the chicken and the puréed mixture into a pot and add the remaining 1½ cups of chicken stock and additional stock if necessary to cover. Simmer 45 minutes, adding more stock if necessary to keep the chicken barely covered. Season to taste with salt. Serve with Thai perfumed rice (see page 16) and lime slices. *Serves 2.*

Cold Poached Coho Salmon with Orange Mayonnaise and Watercress Salad

This is a beautiful and impressive dish. Although it is complicated, all the elements can be prepared ahead (but don't dress the watercress) and painlessly assembled at dinnertime. The recipe makes appetizers for six or a light meal for two.

Coho salmon is hatchery-raised in fresh water. It has a light pink flesh and more flavor than hatchery-raised trout.

One ¾- to 1-pound whole coho salmon

Fumet

Bones from filleted salmon
1 carrot, cut into small dice
1 onion, cut into small dice
1 celery stalk, cut into small dice
1 sprig of thyme or a pinch of dried thyme
½ bay leaf
Parsley
1 quart cold water

Orange Mayonnaise (for salmon)

2 eggs
1 cup olive oil
2 tablespoons fresh orange juice
1 teaspoon orange zest

Orange Dressing (for watercress)

2 tablespoons fresh orange juice
¼ cup light olive oil
Salt and pepper to taste

1 bunch young watercress, washed and drained
1 orange, peeled and cut into wedges

Have the fishmonger fillet the salmon or fillet it yourself; in either case, reserve the bones. Combine the *fumet* ingredients in a large shallow pan and simmer for 1 hour. Strain the fumet. Poach the salmon, filleted into 2 sides, in the simmering fumet for about 3 to 5 minutes. (Add boiling water to cover fish if needed.) The fish should be slightly translucent in the center when done. Carefully remove the fish from the fumet with a slotted spatula and refrigerate immediately.

Prepare the orange mayonnaise. Place the eggs in a blender or food processor and purée briefly. With the motor running, slowly add 1 cup olive oil to beaten eggs. Add the orange juice and orange zest. If the mayonnaise is too thick, thin with a little warm water or cream.

To make the dressing for the watercress, combine the orange juice, olive oil, and salt and pepper.

To serve, dress the watercress with the orange dressing and arrange on a chilled glass plate. Remove the salmon from the refrigerator and place in the center of the watercress, top with the orange mayonnaise, and garnish with the orange wedges. *Serves 2.*

Sautéed Marinated Lamb with Thai Peppers, Red Onion, and Hoisin Sauce

Here is a dish to inspire tears and perspiration! It will serve well as an appetizer or first course, but you should follow it with something soothing and allow some time for the palate to return to normal sensitivity.

¼ cup beef stock
1 tablespoon soy sauce
1 tablespoon minced fresh ginger
3 dried Thai chilies, crumbled
1 bunch cilantro, half chopped and half saved for garnish
7 ounces boned lamb from the leg, sliced across the grain into bite-sized pieces (well-aged meat is preferred)
¼ cup peanut oil
4 to 8 dried Thai chilies (optional)
½ red onion, julienned
½ sweet red pepper, julienned
1 large or 2 small *jalapeño* chilies, julienned
1 tablespoon thinly sliced and julienned young fresh ginger
2½ tablespoons hoisin sauce

Combine the stock, soy sauce, ginger, chilies, and 1 teaspoon of the chopped cilantro and marinate the lamb for 2 hours at room temperature. In a heavy skillet or wok, heat the peanut oil until very hot (almost smoking). Add the Thai chilies and cook for 15 seconds, taking care that they do not burn. (If you prefer the dish spicier, break up the chilies.) Combine the onion, red pepper, jalapeño chilies, and ginger and add to the skillet. Sauté a minute or two more and add the lamb with its marinade. Sauté until nearly done, then add the hoisin sauce and chopped cilantro. Cook another half minute or so and serve with hot rice,* garnished with cilantro. *Serves 2.*

*Christopher prefers Thai perfumed rice; see page 16.

COMPLIMENTS OF THE CHEF

A California landmark, the Claremont Hotel's splendid white Victorian building at the foot of the East Bay hills has overlooked the city of Berkeley for seventy years. Those seven decades have seen dramatic changes in cooking styles, and the Claremont now serves an international cuisine that combines the elements of the New American style with Oriental stir-frying and classic European techniques.

Compliments of

CLAREMONT HOTEL
BERKELEY

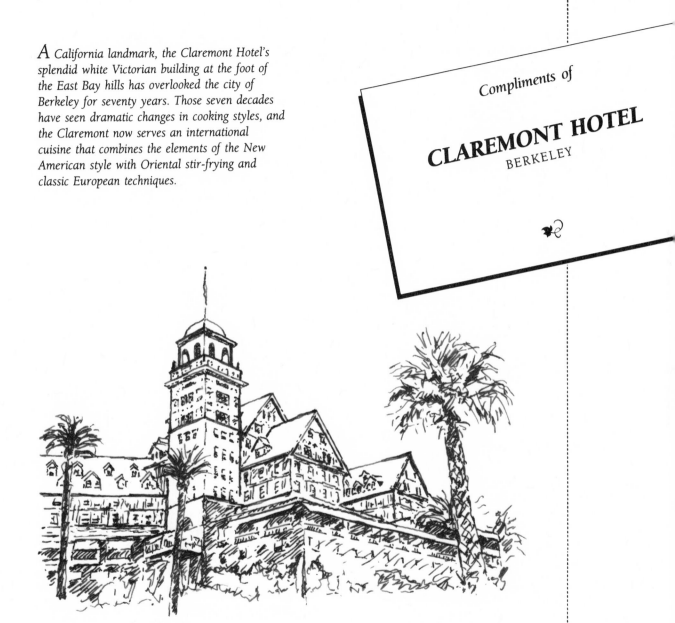

Medallions of Fresh Salmon with Ginger-Cilantro Sauce

Elegant and elaborate, this dish is perfect for a dinner party. Because the flavors are so subtle, impeccably fresh fish is essential.

12 salmon fillets, cut into 2½-ounce strips
Flour
Clarified butter for sautéeing
Fresh mint for garnish

Ginger-Cilantro Sauce

Splash of white wine
2 teaspoons shallots, minced
1 teaspoon fresh ginger, peeled and minced
1 tablespoon cilantro, chopped
6 ounces court bouillon (see page 127 for recipe)
10 ounces béchamel sauce (see page 151 for recipe)
2 teaspoons lemon juice
Salt and pepper to taste

Roll the salmon strips into the shape of a medallion. Lay them flat on the counter and tie the rolls with butcher's string. Flour the medallions lightly and sauté them in clarified butter for 1 minute per side. Remove the salmon and discard the string. Use the pan, unwashed, for the sauce.

To make the sauce, deglaze the pan with the white wine. Add the shallots, ginger, and cilantro and sauté for about 1 minute. Add the court bouillon, béchamel, lemon juice, salt, and pepper. Reduce by half. Strain through a chinoise or cheesecloth.

To serve, cover a dinner plate with a moderate portion of the Ginger-Cilantro Sauce. Lay the salmon gently on the plate and garnish with fresh mint. *Serves 6.*

Chocolate Rendezvous with Crème Anglaise and Raspberry Sauce

This elaborate dessert must be made the day before you intend to serve it and you will need an uninterrupted morning to devote to its many steps. The final product is spectacular. A hint: Use squirt bottles to form the concentric circles of Crème Anglaise and Raspberry Sauce.

Chocolate Pâté

3 tablespoons butter
3 ounces semisweet chocolate, chopped
1 cup heavy cream
4 egg whites
3 tablespoons sugar
12 egg yolks
⅓ cup sugar

Filling

3 egg whites
1 tablespoon sugar
1 pint fresh raspberries

Glaze

6 ounces heavy cream
3½ tablespoons butter
8 ounces semisweet chocolate, chopped

Crème Anglaise

2 cups half and half
½ cup shredded coconut
2 tablespoons vanilla extract
3 egg yolks
¼ cup sugar
3 ounces Grand Marnier liqueur

Raspberry Sauce

1 pint fresh raspberries, and some extra for garnish
1 tablespoon Chambord liqueur

For the Chocolate Pâté, melt the butter and chopped chocolate together. Whip the heavy cream. Beat the egg whites and 3 tablespoons of sugar to soft peaks. Beat the egg yolks with ⅓ cup sugar until thick and add the melted chocolate and butter mixture. Fold in the egg whites and then the whipped cream.

To assemble, pour half the pâté mixture (set the rest aside for later) into a straight-sided loaf pan, measuring 8 by 3 by 3 inches. Freeze until the mixture is solid.

For the Filling, to be added when the pâté is frozen, whip the egg whites and sugar together until stiff peaks form. Wash and dry the raspberries, then fold them into the meringue. Layer the raspberry meringue over the frozen pâté in the loaf pan. Freeze until the meringue is solid.

Fill the pan with the remaining pâté mixture and freeze overnight.

When the loaf is solidly frozen, remove it from pan.

For the Glaze, heat the heavy cream and butter until it boils and then add the chocolate. Cover the loaf with the warm glaze and hold in the freezer until served.

For the Crème Anglaise, heat the half-and-half, coconut, and vanilla in a heavy saucepan over medium heat until very hot. Do not let it boil. Whip the egg yolks with the sugar. Add the hot milk mixture to the yolks and heat in a double boiler for 15 minutes until thickened, stirring constantly. Add the Grand Marnier and strain through a chinoise or fine strainer. Set aside.

For the Raspberry Sauce, purée berries and liqueur in a blender. Pass through a chinoise or a fine strainer to remove seeds. Set aside.

To assemble individual servings, remove the glazed chocolate loaf from the freezer. Pool slightly more than 1 ounce of Crème Anglaise on a 7-inch plate. Form 3 concentric rings of raspberry sauce each 1 inch apart on top of the Crème. With a knife, pull the raspberry sauce toward the edges of the pool, making a feathered star pattern. Place a 1-inch slice of pâté in the center of the pool and garnish with fresh raspberries. *Serves 10 to 12.*

Compliments of

COCOLAT

BERKELEY

Taught to make truffles by her landlady in France, Alice Medrich brought this Gallic skill back to Berkeley and opened Cocolat in 1976, after she could no longer meet the demand for truffles made in her home kitchen. Chocolate-lovers responded to the shop immediately, delighted to be able to purchase these handmade luxuries and a growing number of classic European chocolate desserts as well. The taste for chocolate in the Bay Area has been elevated to a new level with each new creation. One of the best-kept secrets of Cocolat is that the kitchen also produces several wonderful cakes containing no chocolate whatsoever, created for the rare customer who does not subscribe to the prevailing passion.

Queen of California

This rich, elaborate cake, a variation of Reine de Saba, consists of three separate steps and takes a lighter toll on the cook when prepared a day in advance. The cake profits as well, because the glaze seems to need at least a few hours to set up properly. Make sure the cake is completely cooled before glazing. If not, the glaze will never solidify. Oven temperature is also very important.

Cake

3 tablespoons minced dried apricots
¼ cup brandy
6 ounces (6 squares) semisweet or bittersweet baking chocolate, cut into bits
½ cup unsalted butter, cut into pieces
3 large eggs, separated
½ cup plus 3 tablespoons sugar
4 tablespoons all-purpose flour
⅔ cup ground walnuts (about 1 cup before grinding)
Pinch of salt
¼ teaspoon cream of tartar

Caramelized Walnuts

10 perfect walnut halves
½ cup sugar
¼ cup water

Chocolate Glaze

6 ounces (6 squares) semisweet or bittersweet baking chocolate
½ cup unsalted butter, cut into pieces
1 tablespoon corn syrup

To make the cake: Butter and flour an 8-inch round cake pan or line the bottom with waxed or parchment paper. Put the apricots in a small bowl with the brandy and set aside. Melt the chocolate with the butter in a small bowl placed in a pan of not-quite-simmering water. Stir frequently until smooth and melted. Remove from the heat and set aside.

Whisk the yolks and ½ cup of the sugar together until pale yellow. Whisk in the chocolate mixture, flour, and walnuts. Add the steeped apricots and the brandy. Set aside.

In a clean mixer bowl, beat the egg whites, salt, and cream of tartar at high speed until soft peaks are formed. Continue to beat, gradually adding the remaining 3 tablespoons sugar, until firm and glossy. Fold about one-third of the beaten whites into the chocolate batter to lighten it. Fold in the remaining egg whites quickly but gently. Turn the batter into the prepared pan and bake in a preheated 325° oven for 30 to 40 minutes, or until a toothpick inserted about 1 inch from the edge of the cake shows moist crumbs. The center of the cake will test very moist. Set the cake on a rack to cool.

While the cake is baking, prepare the caramelized walnuts: Skewer each walnut on the end of a wooden skewer. Dissolve the sugar and water in a small saucepan over medium heat. Cover and cook 4 to 5 minutes. Uncover, but do not stir. Wash any sugar crystals from the sides of pan with a wet pastry brush. Continue to cook without stirring until the syrup is a medium-dark amber color. Remove from the heat and quickly dip each skewered walnut in the syrup. Set the dipped skewered nuts on the rim of a cake pan to drip, cool, and harden.

While the cake is cooling, make the glaze: Place the chocolate, butter, and corn syrup in a small saucepan and warm gently in a water bath over low heat. Stir until completely melted and smooth. Remove from the heat.

To glaze the cake, cool the glaze until almost set but still spreadable. Run a knife around the edges of the cake in the pan. A cooled cake will have settled in the center, leaving a higher rim around the edges; press these edges down gently with your fingers to flatten and level the cake. Then unmold the cake upside down onto an 8-inch cardboard circle. Spread the edges of the cake with just enough cooled glaze to smooth out any imperfections, cracks, or ragged places. Be careful to keep crumbs out of the glaze pot. Now gently reheat the remaining glaze in the water bath until it is smooth and pourable but not thin and watery. Strain the glaze through a fine strainer. Place the cake on a turntable or plate and pour all of the glaze onto the center of the cake. Use a clean metal spatula to spread the glaze over the edges of the cake. Use as few strokes as possible. Lift the cake up off the plate or turntable (the stiff cardboard circle makes this possible) and set it on a rack.

Remove each caramelized walnut from its skewer, snip off any caramel tails that may have formed, and place the nuts, evenly spaced, around the top of the glazed cake. Allow the glaze to dry before removing the cake to its final serving platter. *Makes one 8-inch cake.*

*F*atapple's serves basic American food—generous hamburgers, apple pie, omelets with home fries, and good thick soups—using high-quality ingredients. Fatapple's burger is one of the best in town, served on a homemade bun. The attached bakery produces volumes of delicious no-nonsense pastries, pies, and muffins, and the restaurant cooks three meals a day, serving hundreds of guests. Just to remind us that this is Berkeley, and not a small town in the Midwest, the owners have covered the walls of the restaurant with Jack London memorabilia.

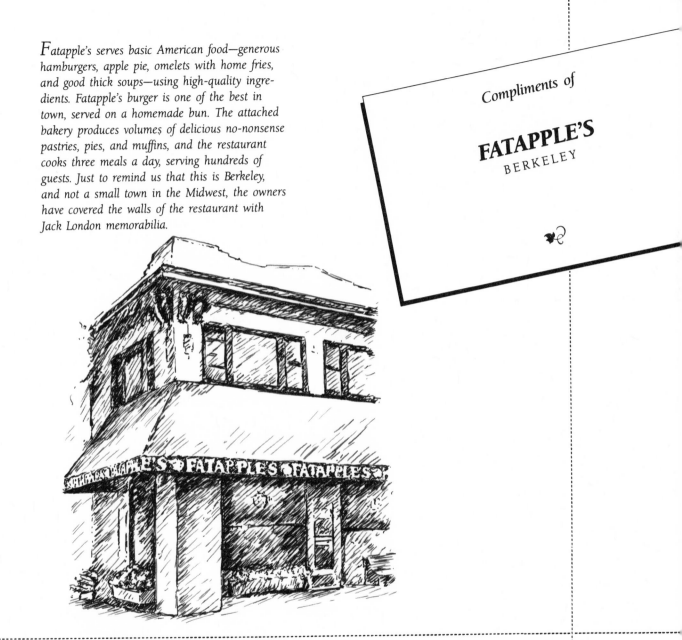

Compliments of

FATAPPLE'S
BERKELEY

Cheese Puffs

For some people in Berkeley, a day that starts without cheese puffs from Fatapple's is a day that should never have started at all. Even if you purchase the puff pastry, this recipe may be tricky to make at home. Be prepared for the possibility that your first batch of cheese puffs may be less than satisfying. Eventually you will achieve success and it will be worth the trouble.

1 pound cream cheese
⅞ cup sugar
1 egg
1½ teaspoons vanilla extract
1½ pounds puff pastry
Powdered sugar

Cream the cheese and sugar together. Add the egg and vanilla and mix until smooth; a blender or food processor is ideal for this. Chill the mixture. Roll out the puff pastry to a thickness of ⅛ inch and cut it into 3-inch squares. Place a heaping teaspoonful of the filling in the center of each square, being careful not to overfill. Pinch the opposite ends of the square together to close, bringing the pinched ends together in the center to form the "puff" shape.

  Place the puffs in small muffin tins. Bake in a preheated 375° oven for 50 minutes, or until the bottoms of the puffs are golden brown. Allow the puffs to cool somewhat, then dust with powdered sugar. *Makes about 4 dozen.*

Chocolate Velvet Pie

Stiffly beaten egg whites are folded into a chocolate custard, then the mixture is chilled in a prebaked pie shell and decorated with whipped cream. An optional method of handling the egg whites would be to omit the sugar from the chocolate custard and add it while beating the egg whites, after soft peaks form. This makes it easier to get stiffly beaten egg whites. The sugar can be increased or decreased to suit your sweet tooth.

½ recipe Pie Dough, following, using ¼ cup
  shortening and ¼ cup butter
1 package (12 ounces) semisweet chocolate
  pieces
¼ cup milk
¼ cup sugar
⅛ teaspoon salt
4 large eggs, separated
1 teaspoon vanilla extract
1 teaspoon instant coffee (high quality)
Whipped cream (optional)

Prepare the pie dough. Roll out the dough ball as in the recipe, and fit it into a 9-inch pie pan. Line the shell with aluminum foil and weight with uncooked beans or rice. Bake in a preheated 400° oven for 10 to 15 minutes. or until the shell has dried out and holds its shape. Remove the foil and beans or rice, reduce heat to 350°, and bake until brown, 15 to 20 minutes.

continued

Combine the chocolate, milk, sugar, salt, egg yolks, vanilla, and instant coffee in the top of a double boiler. Cook over hot water until the mixture is blended and smooth. Cool slightly. Beat the egg whites until stiff peaks form. Fold the egg whites into the chocolate mixture, blending well. Pour into the cool pie shell. Chill at least 2 or 3 hours. To serve, decorate with a border of whipped cream. *Serves 8.*

Pecan Pie

This is a good, old-fashioned pecan pie, simple to make and sure to please.

½ recipe Pie Dough, following
¾ cup pecan halves
3 large eggs, beaten slightly
¾ cup sugar
¾ cup dark corn syrup
¼ teaspoon salt
1 teaspoon vanilla extract
3 tablespoons cooled melted butter

Prepare one 9-inch uncooked pie shell and refrigerate 30 minutes or overnight. Toast the pecans in a 300° oven for 5 minutes. Mix all the remaining ingredients until well blended. Put the pecans into the pie shell. Pour the filling into the shell on top of the pecans. The pecans should be well covered with filling; they will float to the top while cooking. Bake in a preheated 350° oven for 1 hour, or until the pie is nicely browned and set. *Makes 6 to 8 servings.*

Pie Dough

3 cups all-purpose unbleached flour
¼ teaspoon salt
¾ cup shortening
¼ cup unsalted butter
2 to 4 tablespoons cold water

Combine the flour and salt in a mixing bowl. Cut in the shortening and butter with a pastry blender or 2 knives until the mixture is the consistency of tiny peas. Sprinkle with the cold water, 1 tablespoon at a time, tossing the mixture lightly and stirring with a fork. Add water each time to the driest part of the mixture. Use only enough water to make the dough hold together when pressed gently with a fork. It should not be sticky.

Shape the dough into 2 smooth balls. Wrap in waxed paper and refrigerate at least 30 minutes or until ready to fill and bake pie.

On a lightly floured surface, press 1 dough ball into a flat circle with your hands. Roll it lightly with short strokes from the center in all directions to a ⅛-inch thickness, making a 10-inch to 11-inch circle. Fold the rolled dough in half and ease it loosely into the pie pan with the fold in the center. Unfold and fit into the pan, using care not to stretch the dough. Gently press out any air pockets with your fingertips. Make sure there are no openings for juices to escape. To fill and bake, see individual recipes. *Makes dough for a 9-10-inch double-crust pie.*

Fourth Street Grill combines what is now considered classic Berkeley cuisine with the hearty cooking of Mexico and the Southwest. The result is a variety of dishes ranging from hamburgers to Louisiana sausages, often featuring the shoestring potatoes that have become a trademark of the restaurant. The Fourth Street Grill has helped turn a formerly industrial area into one filled with fashionable boutiques. Some of the area's best chefs, including Mark Miller and Amy Shaw, have made their home at owner Susie Nelson's landmark establishment.

Roasted Tomato and Chili Soup

A simple soup with clean, clear flavors. If poblano chilies are not available, use any large mild green chili; Italian green chilies will even work in a pinch, but avoid the standard green bell pepper. If you want the soup spicier, include a jalapeño or serrano chili (or two). Queso fresco is a mild white Mexican cheese with a tang unduplicated elsewhere. If you can't get it, substitute Parmesan or dry Monterey jack cheese.

8 large vine-ripened tomatoes, cored
6 large fresh poblano chilies
1 large white onion, cut into thin slices
2 garlic cloves, minced
1 bunch cilantro, tied together
¼ cup virgin olive oil
6 cups rich chicken stock
6 corn tortillas
Peanut oil
¼ cup fresh lime juice
Salt and pepper to taste
1 lime, cut in slices
Grated queso fresco
Cilantro sprigs

Char the tomatoes over an open gas flame, a charcoal grill, or under a broiler until they are soft and the skins are well browned. Do not discard the blackened parts. Chop the tomatoes finely or semi-purée them in a blender or food processor.

Roast, peel, and seed the chilies (see Basics). Cut the chilies into strips. Sauté the onion, garlic, and cilantro in the olive oil over low heat. Add 1 cup of the chicken stock, cover the pan, and let the mixture steam for about 20 minutes. Add the chili strips, tomatoes, and the remainder of the chicken stock. Cook for 10 minutes.

Meanwhile, cut the tortillas into ⅜-inch-wide strips and fry in ¼ inch of peanut oil. Remove from the pan with a slotted spoon and drain on paper towels. Finally, season the soup with lime juice, salt, and pepper. Remove the bunch of cilantro just before serving. Garnish the soup with the strips of fried corn tortillas, a slice of lime, some grated queso fresco, and sprigs of cilantro. *Serves 4 to 6.*

San Remo Pasta with Roasted Tomatoes and Black Olives

This is a pasta with pronounced flavors: imported black olives, sun-dried tomatoes, red pepper flakes, and strong olive oil. It is delicious and easy to prepare, but should not be served with foods that it will overwhelm. Roasting the tomatoes gives them a slightly caramelized flavor and removes excess moisture. If the tomatoes are still very wet after roasting, cook them longer in the olive oil before adding the other ingredients. Use plain egg pasta if you can't find red pepper pasta.

2 pounds tomatoes
½ cup fruity virgin olive oil
2 large garlic cloves, or 2 teaspoons minced garlic
½ teaspoon dried red pepper flakes
50 imported small black olives, pitted
3 ounces sun-dried tomatoes
Basil leaves
¾ pound fresh red pepper pasta
Freshly grated Parmesan cheese, preferably Italian

Roast the tomatoes in a preheated 400° oven for 30 minutes. In a large skillet or sauté pan, heat the olive oil with 3 cups of the roasted tomatoes and bring to a boil. Add the garlic, red pepper flakes, olives, and sun-dried tomatoes, and cook for a few minutes until the garlic has lost its raw taste. Add the basil and turn off the heat.

In a large amount of boiling salted water, cook the pasta for 2 to 3 minutes, or until *al dente*. Remove the pasta from the water, drain, and toss with the sauce, coating the pasta thoroughly. Serve with freshly grated Parmesan. *Serves 2 to 4.*

Seafood is the unifying theme for this restaurant, but its variations are infinite. Gertie's was opened by John Shields, formerly a chef at À La Carte, who named the restaurant after his grandmother. The present owner is Mr. Kim and the chef is Eric Haines. Gertie's offers a number of different regional American dishes and, as a result, one can sample East Coast and Southern dishes not ordinarily available in Berkeley. Seafood is flown in daily from the East and Gulf coasts and supplemented with fresh local ingredients, an unbeatable combination.

Compliments of

GERTIE'S
CHESAPEAKE BAY CAFÉ
BERKELEY

Chicken Liver Mousse Pâté

*T*his decadently rich liver pâté works well as a spread for good bread or crackers and would fit well in a cocktail setting or be good with apéritifs. It is really a little rich to be an integral part of a menu. Be sure to make this a day ahead of time and serve it chilled.

1 small onion, chopped
2 tablespoons chopped shallots
2½ cups (5 sticks) unsalted butter
1 pound chicken livers
½ cup dry Marsala wine
1 tablespoon dried thyme, crumbled
Salt and pepper to taste
¾ cup heavy cream

Sauté the onion and shallots in 1 cup (2 sticks) of the butter until soft. Add the chicken livers and cook for 3 minutes. Then add the Marsala, thyme, salt, and pepper. Continue to cook until the livers are brown but still pink inside and the alcohol is cooked off.

With a slotted spoon, transfer the livers into a blender or a food processor. Mix until very smooth. Cut the remaining butter into small pieces and add to the mixture slowly. When the butter is incorporated, add the cream. The mixture will seem quite liquid.

Pour the mixture into a pâté or standard-sized loaf pan and chill for 24 hours. To unmold, set the pan in a larger pan of hot water, run a knife around the edge of the pâté, and turn the pâté out onto a plate. *Makes 6 cups, or 3 pounds.*

Chocolate Bourbon Pecan Pie

A luscious variation on the pecan pie theme, this is a rich and very sweet conclusion to a meal.

½ recipe Pie Dough, page 83
3 eggs, lightly beaten
1 cup brown sugar
1 cup dark corn syrup
¼ cup flour
3 ounces (3 squares) unsweetened chocolate, broken into pieces
¼ cup bourbon
½ cup unsalted butter, cut into pieces
¼ cup pecan halves

Prepare the pie dough. Roll out the dough ball as in the recipe, and fit it into a 9-inch pie pan. Line the shell with aluminum foil and weight with uncooked beans or rice. Place in a preheated 350° oven until dry but not brown, about 20 minutes.

Cream the eggs and brown sugar together. Add the corn syrup and flour. Melt the chocolate in a double boiler with the bourbon. When completely melted, add the butter. Pour the chocolate mixture into the egg mixture and mix well. Pour this mixture into the pie shell, arrange the pecan halves on top, and bake in a preheated 300° oven for 1 hour and 10 minutes, or until well browned and slightly puffed. *Makes 6 to 8 servings.*

Giovanni's is the culmination of the classic immigrant story: owner John Schipani transformed a small shop selling pizza by the slice into this full-scale restaurant serving a broad range of Italian cuisine. Basic hearty Italian fare is available on a daily basis, with a nod to new Italian dishes and ingredients such as Carpaccio and sun-dried tomatoes. Special monthly wine dinners showcase the efforts of local vintners. Giovanni's is a Berkeley institution where you can still find spaghetti and pizza, as well as dishes drawn from the "new" Italian cuisine.

Compliments of

GIOVANNI'S
BERKELEY

Roasted Garlic and Almond Spread

A simple spread for crackers, bread sticks, or raw vegetables—good with cocktails or apéritifs.

3 tablespoons unblanched almonds
12 garlic cloves, peeled
3 tablespoons peanut oil
8 ounces cream cheese, at room temperature
¼ cup sour cream
1 teaspoon Worcestershire sauce
1 teaspoon Dijon mustard
2 tablespoons chopped fresh parsley
1 teaspoon dried rosemary
2 shallots, chopped
Salt and pepper to taste
⅓ cup heavy cream

Toast the almonds in a preheated 325° oven for 10 minutes; chop. Lower the heat to 275° and bake the garlic in the oil for about 40 minutes, until the cloves are tender but not browned. You may have to cover the garlic to prevent browning. Let the garlic cool, then blend it with the oil in a food processor. Add the cream cheese, sour cream, Worcestershire sauce, and mustard and blend thoroughly. Then add the almonds, parsley, rosemary, shallots, salt, and pepper. Blend again.

Remove the spread from the food processor and place in a mixing bowl. Whip the cream and fold it into the mixture. Pour the spread into a serving bowl, chill for 2 hours, and serve at room temperature. *Makes about 1½ cups.*

Red Pesto

A simple but interesting recipe for pasta, chicken, or fish, which can be adjusted to your taste by the addition of lemon or lime juice, more garlic or less, stronger olive oil, or the addition of herbs or chilies.

4 red bell peppers
⅓ cup almonds
⅓ cup pine nuts
5 Roma (plum) tomatoes, peeled and seeded
3 garlic cloves
1 teaspoon salt
1 cup olive oil
⅛ teaspoon cayenne
½ cup heavy cream (optional)
½ cup freshly grated Parmesan cheese (optional)

Roast, peel, and seed the peppers (see Basics). Toast the almonds and pine nuts in a preheated 300° oven for 5 to 10 minutes.

Blend the peppers, toasted nuts, tomatoes, garlic, salt, olive oil, and cayenne thoroughly in a blender or food processor and taste for salt. To serve the sauce with broiled fish or chicken, add the cream. For pasta, add the Parmesan cheese. *Makes 2 cups, or enough for 3 pounds of pasta.*

In the heart of a district slated for urban renewal, the Gulf Coast Oyster Bar has beaten the pace of redevelopment by several years. The area is coming to life, and Gulf Coast provides a culinary landmark. Run by Dan Wormhoult and his wife, Carolyn, a native of New Orleans, the Gulf Coast offers andouille, oysters, and shrimp from New Orleans, as well as fresh oysters and fish from the East and West coasts.

Compliments of

GULF COAST OYSTER BAR

OAKLAND

Tartar Sauce

*How typical of a Bay Area restaurant to take
something decidedly American, tartar sauce, back
to its roots,* Sauce gribiche, *then add an unusual
ingredient or two and even put it to an unusual
use. And don't approach this sauce lightly. It is
an emulsion based on hard-cooked egg yolks,
which are far more reluctant to absorb oil than
are raw yolks. Thorough beating and very gradual additions of oil are the keys to success here.
The directions are given for hand mixing, but a
food processor will prove helpful. All the ingredients should be at room temperature.*

1 tablespoon Balsamic vinegar
¾ teaspoon white wine vinegar
¾ teaspoon lemon juice
1 tablespoon parsley, chopped
Half a bunch chervil, chopped
1 tablespoon tarragon, chopped
3 hard-cooked egg yolks
¾ to 1 cup extra-virgin olive oil
3 hard-cooked egg whites, julienned
⅓ cup cornichons, drained, rinsed, and
  minced
½ shallot, minced
½ tablespoon yellow onion, minced
1 tablespoon capers, drained and rinsed
⅛ cup whole-grain mustard
Salt and pepper

Combine the vinegars and lemon juice. Finely
chop the parsley, chervil, and tarragon and, if
you don't want the sauce to turn green, put
the herbs in a towel and rinse and squeeze
them dry. If the herbs are not rinsed they will
give a stronger flavor to the sauce.

In a nonreactive mixing bowl, mash the egg
yolks to a paste with half the vinegar and
lemon juice mixture and the mustard until absolutely smooth. Drizzle in a small quantity of
oil, while beating constantly. When it is well
absorbed, slowly add more oil. As the sauce
thickens, add more of the vinegar and lemon
juice mixture to keep it at the proper consistency. When all the oil is added, fold in the
remaining ingredients.

If the sauce separates, begin a standard
mayonnaise in a clean bowl by beating 1 egg
yolk well, adding a few drops of vinegar and,
while beating, slowly drizzling in ¼ cup of
oil. When the emulsion is well established,
gradually add the broken sauce and complete
the recipe where you left off. *Makes about 2
cups.*

Leek Terrine with Achiote Vinaigrette Appetizer

Leeks contain a small amount of gelatin. When they are cooked, then packed into a terrine and chilled, they form a coherent, sliceable mold. The green and white of leeks may be accented by adding a layer of roasted red or yellow peppers, golden beets, or other seasonal vegetables.

2 yellow onions
4 stalks celery
1 bottle dry white wine
1 bunch parsley
2 bay leaves
5 black peppercorns
4 bunches leeks

Achiote Vinaigrette

2 cups virgin olive oil
½ cup achiote seeds, lightly rinsed (these can be purchased in Mexican groceries)
¾ cup Balsamic vinegar
1 egg yolk
3 cloves garlic
2 tablespoons fresh herbs, thyme or marjoram, chopped

To make a poaching liquid for the leeks, chop the onions and celery coarsely and place them, with the wine, parsley, bay leaves, and peppercorns, in a nonreactive pot large enough to hold the trimmed leeks without crowding. Fill the pot with water and simmer for 45 minutes.

Strain and reserve the broth. Meanwhile, prepare the leeks. Split them in half lengthwise and wash well to remove all grit. Trim off the root end and cut the leeks to fit your casserole, which should be a deep, narrow 8-cup loaf pan.

Tie the leeks into four bundles and poach them in the strained broth for 15 minutes. Drain the leeks, untie the bundles and, when they are cool enough to handle, layer them into the casserole, which has been lined with plastic wrap. Alternate the layers by switching the white ends back and forth. Weight the terrine and refrigerate overnight.

Make the Achiote Vinaigrette a few hours before you plan to serve the terrine as the flavor improves over time. In a stainless steel saucepan, heat the olive oil and the achiote seeds over medium heat until simmering and cook for 2 minutes. Immediately strain the oil as it will continue to color and flavor as it cools and will turn bitter if cooked too long.

In a bowl whisk the Balsamic vinegar with the egg yolk. Add the oil gradually, whisking to emulsify it. When all the oil is incorporated, stir in the whole garlic and herbs. Salt and pepper as necessary.

To serve, line the plates with the vinaigrette. Gently slice the terrine with a serrated knife and place in the dressing. *Serves 8.*

Compliments of

HUNAN PALACE

ALBANY

*O*wner-chef Herman Chang worked for seven years at Ghirardelli Square's famous Mandarin Restaurant in San Francisco before opening his own place in Berkeley. A member of an established restaurant family (relatives of his own two other restaurants), Mr. Chang includes several of China's many cuisines in his menu, from the robust spicy cooking of Hunan and Szechwan in the west to the delicate subtleties of Peking cuisine in the north.

Eggplant with Spicy Garlic Sauce

You can lessen the chili content, but the dish won't be the same. It should come and get you. The bland eggplant is a good foil for the forthright flavors of other ingredients.

1 eggplant (approximately 1 pound)
Peanut oil for deep-frying
1 teaspoon sugar
1½ tablespoons rice vinegar
1 tablespoon soy sauce
2 teaspoons dry sherry
1 cup chicken broth
3 tablespoons peanut oil
5 dried red peppers
1½ tablespoons minced garlic
1 teaspoon minced fresh ginger
1 tablespoon cornstarch, diluted in
   2 tablespoons water
1 teaspoon Oriental sesame oil
Chopped green onions

Cut the eggplant into finger-sized slices. Heat the oil to a depth of 1 inch in a sauté pan or skillet until it begins to smoke on the sides. Put one-half of the eggplant in and fry until golden brown and soft (approximately 3 minutes). Remove with a slotted spoon and drain on paper towels, pressing the eggplant to squeeze out excess oil. Cook the remaining eggplant and set all aside.

In a small bowl, mix together the sugar, rice vinegar, soy sauce, sherry, and chicken broth; set aside.

Heat the 3 tablespoons oil in a clean pan. Add the peppers and cook a few seconds; stir to prevent burning. Add the garlic and ginger and cook a few seconds more. Add the liquid mixture and bring to a boil. Add the eggplant and cook about 1 minute, or until the sauce is reduced. Mix in the cornstarch to thicken the sauce. Add the sesame oil. Stir until heated through. Sprinkle with the chopped onion. *Serves 4.*

Bon Bon Chicken

This makes a fairly rich but easily executed first course. The sometimes hard-to-find Szechwan peppercorns can be replaced with ground white pepper, or omitted.

1 whole chicken breast, halved
½ tablespoon sesame seeds
1 tablespoon creamy peanut butter
1 tablespoon sesame seed paste
2 tablespoons distilled vinegar
1 tablespoon soy sauce
½ teaspoon salt
1½ tablespoons sugar
1 tablespoon medium-dry sherry
  (amontillado)
1 tablespoon "hot oil"* (chili oil)
½ teaspoon ground Szechwan peppercorns
1 teaspoon Oriental sesame oil
2 zucchini, cut in fine julienne
1 tablespoon chopped fresh cilantro

Place the chicken in a saucepan, add water to cover, and bring to a simmer; cover and cook until tender, about 5 to 7 minutes. Remove the chicken from the pan with a slotted spoon; cool. Remove the meat from the bones and cut into bite-sized pieces. Set aside.

Toast the sesame seeds 2 to 3 minutes in a preheated 300° oven; set aside. Put the peanut butter and sesame seed paste in a small bowl and soften over boiling water. Add the next 8 ingredients. Mix well.

Arrange the julienned zucchini on a platter, put the shredded chicken on top, and pour the seasoning sauce evenly over all. Sprinkle with the sesame seeds and cilantro. *Serves 4 as a main course, 6 to 8 as an appetizer.*

*"Hot oil" is made by adding 1 tablespoon dried red pepper flakes to 1 cup of very hot peanut oil, allowing it to cool, and then straining the oil. It is sometimes available bottled in Chinese markets.

This restaurant just outside Berkeley's city limits is owned and managed by three women who met while working together as probation officers for Alameda County. They still hold professional positions while they combine their culinary talents. Jackie Karkazis bakes the pastries and the wonderful biscuits that are the stars of the breakfast menu; Sharon Lazaneo does all the dinner cooking; and Kathy Davisson specializes in soups and salads. Inn Kensington was designed to serve the neighborhood, but people now come from all over the Berkeley area to enjoy country-style cooking emphasizing freshness.

Compliments of

INN KENSINGTON
KENSINGTON

Orange, Red Onion, and Avocado Salad with Walnut Oil Dressing

A salad that lends itself to dramatic presentation. The walnut oil dressing ties all the elements together successfully.

Dressing

¼ cup fresh lemon juice
½ teaspoon Dijon mustard
Salt and pepper to taste
¾ cup walnut oil (use 1 cup if a less tart dressing is desired)

¾ cup walnuts
3 oranges
2 heads butter lettuce, cored and separated
1 medium red onion, thinly sliced
1 large or 2 small avocados, peeled and sliced
24 black olives

To prepare the dressing, combine the lemon juice, mustard, salt, and pepper. Mix well and add the walnut oil.

Toast the walnuts in a preheated 325° oven for 7 minutes. Peel the oranges, removing as much of the bitter white rind as possible; slice into rounds. Toss the lettuce with dressing and distribute the lettuce among 6 plates. Arrange the orange slices, red onion slices, avocado slices, and olives on the lettuce. Sprinkle with the walnuts. Drizzle the dressing on top. *Serves 6.*

Salmon with Fresh Basil Butter

A fine example of one of the area's characteristic treatments of good fresh fish. The composed butter is very clean and simple; don't expect it to make up for inferior fish.

Basil Butter

1 cup (2 sticks) unsalted butter, at room temperature
2 bunches basil, leaves only, minced
2 teaspoons Dijon mustard
2 tablespoons fresh lemon juice
Pinch of salt

Eight ¼- to ½-pound salmon fillets

Place all the basil butter ingredients into a blender or food processor and purée until blended. This may take as long as 5 minutes and will result in a smooth green butter.

Bake or broil the salmon fillets for 7 to 10 minutes (450° for baking), depending on thickness (they should be slightly translucent in the center). Top each fillet with about 2 tablespoons of basil butter and serve immediately. *Serves 8.*

In response to the growth of new businesses in Emeryville and the paucity of restaurants, Kathleen de Wilbur has leased the front office space of the General Motors Parts warehouse and turned it into a fifties-style open-kitchen café. On sunny days, sidewalk tables and umbrellas are set out by the newly tree-lined street. The menu, mainly soups and sandwiches, offers freshness, high quality, and hearty portions.

Compliments of

KATHLEEN'S DOYLE STREET CAFÉ
EMERYVILLE

Fresh Fruit Bran Muffins

*F*resh strawberries and bananas are Doyle Street staples. Muffins flavored with bananas, blueberries, and walnuts are wonderful in the summer. For holiday baking, cranberry, banana, and walnut muffins would be a good choice. The strawberries in the recipe below may be replaced by a cup of fruit and nuts in any combination.

2¼ cups bran
1¾ cups milk
2¼ cups flour
3½ teaspoons baking powder
1 teaspoon salt
½ cup (1 stick) butter, softened
½ cup sugar
½ cup molasses
2 eggs
1 cup fresh strawberries

Preheat the oven to 400°. Combine the bran and milk and let the mixture stand for 10 minutes. In a separate bowl, combine the flour, baking powder, and salt.

Cream together the butter, sugar, molasses, and eggs and then add the bran and milk mixture. Stir in the strawberries. Fold this mixture into the dry ingredients, being careful not to overmix.

Spoon into buttered muffin tins and bake for approximately 30 minutes, or until golden brown. *Makes about 30 muffins.*

Spicy Toasted Sesame Sauce

*T*his is also known as "Special Sauce" at the Doyle Street Café, where it is served with roast beef sandwiches. Be sure that the sesame seeds are sizzling hot when they are added to the sauce as it is this that makes the sauce especially flavorful.

About 2 cups basic mayonnaise
¼ cup horseradish
¼ cup Tabasco sauce
¼ cup Worcestershire sauce
2 or 3 cloves garlic, minced
⅓ cup sesame seeds

Blend all the ingredients, except the sesame seeds, thoroughly. Toast in a dry frying pan. When the seeds are brown, popping, and hot, add them to the mayonnaise mixture. *Makes almost 3 cups.*

Joanne's Pickles

These pickles can take on a personality of the creator's choosing. Joanne says, "I prefer [these pickles] spicy and hot, and sometimes will pour the various peppers into the nonreactive container in hopes of that end."

7½ pounds pickling cucumbers
10 cups water
10 cups white vinegar
1⅓ cups kosher salt
10 cloves garlic*
2 bunches fresh dill
2 tablespoons crushed red pepper
2 tablespoons whole black pepper
2 tablespoons whole white pepper
1 tablespoon whole allspice
1 red onion, thinly sliced

Wash the cucumbers thoroughly and let them soak in a sink of ice water.

In a noncorrosive saucepan, over medium heat, boil the water, vinegar, salt, and garlic.

Towel-dry the cucumbers and layer them, in a nonreactive container, with the fresh dill. Add the pepper, allspice, and onion. When the garlic in the brine is soft, pour the brine over the cucumbers. Weight the mixture down so that all the cucumbers are submerged and let it stand overnight. *Makes about 8 pounds.*

*The amount of garlic regulates the sweetness of the pickles; the more garlic, the more "buttery" the pickle.

NOTE: The quantities of black, white, and red pepper may be increased according to taste.

The owners of La Crème de la Crème, David and Kathy Nugent, opened this charming, romantic restaurant in an old Victorian house in 1983. When they remodelled the building, David discovered a copy of the San Francisco Chronicle dated 1893. The food is innovative French cuisine for which classical bases provide a foundation for new and delicious dishes.

Eggplant "Cake" with Tomato "Jelly"

This is not a sweet but a terrine that, when finished, looks like a chocolate cake with raspberry filling. It makes a lovely first course.

1½ pounds Japanese eggplant
¼ cup olive oil plus extra for sautéeing
1 pound tomatoes, peeled, seeded, and diced
2 cloves garlic
Salt and pepper
3 eggs, lightly beaten
½ cup freshly grated Parmesan cheese
3 tablespoons chopped parsley

Cut the eggplants in half lengthwise. Sauté them in hot olive oil, cut-side down, until they are tender, about 6 to 8 minutes. They will tend to scorch, so watch the heat carefully. Keep enough oil in the pan so that the eggplants are always moist and do not stick. They will cook faster with a cover and not need as much oil. Do not turn them over. When the eggplants are tender, remove and cool.

Cook the diced tomatoes with one whole garlic clove in ¼ cup olive oil over medium heat until all the water from the tomatoes has evaporated, about 20 minutes. Remove the garlic, skim off the excess oil, and season to taste with the salt and pepper.

When the eggplant has cooled, gently remove the flesh from the skin with a spoon, chop it coarsely, and mix it with the eggs, cheese, parsley, and the remaining garlic clove, which has been finely minced. Season with salt and pepper. Reserve the eggplant skins.

Oil an 8-cup loaf pan with olive oil, line the bottom with the eggplant skins, skin-side down. Spread half the eggplant mixture over this and cover with all of the tomato sauce. Follow with the remaining eggplant mixture, being careful not to disarrange the tomato layer. Finally, top the terrine with a layer of eggplant skins, skin-side up.

Cover with oiled aluminum foil and bake in a hot water bath at 350° until set, 45 minutes to an hour. Allow to set for 15 minutes, then run a knife around the edges to loosen. Unmold by inverting the loaf onto a serving platter. *Serves 6 to 8.*

Apple Tart "Ma Mère"

This is a first rate apple tart. It harks back to the apple tarts made by the chef's mother, who used nutmeg, never cinnamon.

Crème Pâtissière

1¾ cups milk
Half a vanilla bean
½ cup sugar
5 egg yolks
¼ cup flour or cornstarch

Sweet Pastry Shell

1⅓ cups flour
8 tablespoons (1 stick) butter, cold and cut
   into small pieces
4 tablespoons sugar
1 small egg
1 teaspoon orange flower water

Apple Filling

1 cup sugar
2 cups water
Half a vanilla bean
6 green cooking apples

To make the Crème Pâtissière, cut the vanilla bean in half lengthwise, scrape the seeds out into the milk in a saucepan, toss in the scraped-out half of the vanilla bean, and bring the mixture to a boil. Cover and allow to steep for 20 minutes.

Beat the egg yolks and sugar until pale and, when lifted, drops in a ribbon from the beaters. Fold in the flour and gradually whisk in the hot milk.

Return the custard to the saucepan and bring to a boil. Cook gently for a few minutes until the flour has lost its raw flavor, stirring constantly to prevent scorching. Remove the vanilla bean.

To make the Pastry Shell, mix the flour and sugar. Cut the butter into the flour with your fingertips. Do not overmix. Add the egg and the orange flower water. Mix generously until blended. Chill for 1 hour.

Roll out the dough to fit the tart pan, cover it with aluminum foil, weight with beans or pie weights, and bake at 400°. When the pastry is dried out, remove the foil and continue baking until golden brown. The sugar content makes this pastry likely to scorch, so watch it carefully.

For the Apple Filling, make a syrup of the sugar, water, and vanilla bean, split lengthwise and scraped of seeds. Add both seeds and bean to syrup. Boil. Peel, quarter, and core the apples. Put the fruit into the boiling syrup and return to the boil. Cover and remove from heat. Let the mixture stand until the apples are barely soft, usually 5 to 10 minutes. Pour into a bowl and let the apples cool in the syrup.

To assemble the tart, spread the pastry cream about ½ inch thick on the baked and cooled tart shell. Drain the syrup from the poached apples, slice them uniformly, and arrange them decoratively on the pastry cream. Grate nutmeg all over the fruit. *Serves 8.*

*L*alime's opened on Solano Avenue in 1985 and quickly found a home in the Berkeley food scene. It offers an innovative mixture of French and Cambodian cuisine with a dash of the Middle East added by its Armenian owners. Lalime is the French-Cambodian name of the wife of one of the owners. Lalime's recently moved to its present Gilman Street address where it has expanded dining and kitchen facilities. In its old space on Solano Avenue, Lalime's has opened a quality take-out deli and lunch spot called Thyme Wise.

Compliments of

LALIME'S
BERKELEY

Marinated Grilled Leg of Lamb

This very interesting and delicious grilled dish has its roots in Middle Eastern cuisines and is well worth some extra trouble to find the exotic ingredients. A two- to three-day marinating period is very important as the acidic properties of the sumac and pomegranate have a tenderizing and penetrating effect on the meat.

The meat should be from the widest part of the leg and in single muscle groups as much as possible. If this is not possible, use boneless 1½-inch slices from the sirloin end of the lamb leg. This marinade also works well on a butterflied, boneless leg of lamb, which should be allowed to marinate for 4 or 5 days because of the thickness of the meat.

3 pounds leg of lamb
1 teaspoon ground cloves
1 teaspoon ground cinnamon
1 teaspoon ground cumin
1 teaspoon ground coriander
1 teaspoon ground fennel
1 tablespoon sumac (available at Middle Eastern groceries)
1 tablespoon paprika
1 teaspoon pepper, freshly ground
1 teaspoon salt
2 tablespoons Balsamic vinegar
2 tablespoons soy sauce
1 tablespoon minced garlic
1 pomegranate (juice on a citrus juicer, or use ½ cup bottled pomegranate juice)
1 cup extra-virgin olive oil

Combine the spices, salt, pepper, vinegar, soy sauce, and garlic and rub the mixture into the meat for 2 minutes until the mixture has penetrated the meat and turned it a reddish color. Add the pomegranate juice and olive oil and rub into the meat to coat it thoroughly. Marinate for 2 or 3 days.

To cook, grill over a medium charcoal fire and serve rare or medium-rare. *Serves 6.*

Stuffed Pasilla Chili

Because it is spicy, this is a warming dish, very suitable as an accompaniment to plain roasts and grills—the sort of dish one thinks of to serve in winter, when fresh corn isn't available. Corn, however, takes very well to freezing. At the height of summer, cut the kernels off the freshest corn you can find and freeze them.

10 large *pasilla* chilies
5 ears fresh corn
5 scallions, finely chopped
1 bunch cilantro (½ cup, packed)
¾ cup diced *tomatillos*
6 ounces Jack cheese, grated
6 ounces sharp Cheddar cheese, grated
½ teaspoon cayenne
1 teaspoon paprika
Salt and pepper to taste
Lemon juice to taste

Grill or roast the chilies, turning until all sides are charred. Then put them in a pan, cover with foil, and set aside to cool. Peel the chilies gently by hand and open, by cutting the chilies lengthwise once, to take out the seeds. Rinse under cold water to get rid of any loose skin and seeds. Wrap the chilies in a kitchen towel to dry.

Cook the corn and cut the kernels off with a paring knife. Put all the ingredients (except the chilies) in a large bowl and mix by hand until you have an even mixture. Season with salt, pepper, and lemon juice. Stuff the chilies and wrap them individually in aluminum foil coated with olive oil. Put the wrapped peppers in a baking dish and cook in a preheated oven at 425° for 15 minutes. To serve, take the foil off and gently slide the peppers onto a plate. *Serves 6.*

LIPPZ BISTRO
CONCORD

Dayna Elkins, who is both chef and owner, and her mother, Patti Doster, work together on all aspects of the operation of this semi-casual but sophisticated restaurant. Lippz Bistro is in one of Concord's oldest houses in an unlikely setting of banks and office buildings. The cuisine is international and includes a tapas-style happy hour on weekdays.

Grilled Swordfish with Chili-Cumin Butter

A staple of California grill restaurants is a dish of perfectly fresh fish, grilled and served with a flavorful composed butter. The corn pudding recipe that follows is a perfect complement to the grilled fish.

Chili-Cumin Butter

3 cloves garlic
1 shallot, peeled
2 teaspoons cumin seeds, toasted in a dry pan until fragrant
3 *pasilla* or Anaheim chili peppers, roasted, peeled, and cooled
Juice of 1 small lime
Salt and pepper to taste
1 cup unsalted butter, at room temperature
½ cup cilantro leaves, finely chopped

4 swordfish steaks, 6 to 8 ounces each
Olive oil

Make the composed butter first. Chop the garlic and the shallot in a processor or blender. Crush the cumin seeds with a mortar and pestle or in coffee and spice grinder and add to processor with the roasted peppers, lime juice, salt, pepper, and softened butter. Process in short spurts until combined well.

Spread the butter onto parchment paper or foil in a rectangular shape. Fold paper over until the ends meet and scrape the butter to the center of the fold with a spatula. Twist the ends of the paper so that the butter forms a sausage shape; freeze until firm, about half an hour. Remove the paper and roll the butter in chopped cilantro to cover.

Brush the fish with olive oil and grill over coals or in a ridged cast-iron pan until done to your taste. Top with Chili-Cumin Butter, sliced into 1-inch thick slices and placed on the hot fish fillets. *Serves 4.*

Southwestern Corn and Cheddar "Pudding"

A side dish, this "pudding" is excellent with grilled fish and also with chicken and spicy meat dishes.

5 cups corn kernels
½ cup butter, softened
¾ cup cornmeal
3 tablespoons sugar
3 ounces cream cheese
1 teaspoon salt
⅓ cup cream
8 ounces Cheddar cheese, grated
½ cup chopped *pasilla* or Anaheim chilies, roasted (see Basics for roasting method)

Diablo Mousse Cake

This cake was created for singer Jesse Colin Young, who had a craving for a dense, intensely chocolate cake. This one does not contain flour owing to the singer's allergy to wheat.

Crust

3 tablespoons butter
4 ounces semisweet chocolate
½ teaspoon almond extract
1 cup almonds, toasted and chopped

Purée 4 cups of the corn kernels in a processor. Beat the butter in a mixing bowl until fluffy. Beat in the cornmeal, sugar, cream cheese, and salt. Stir in the corn purée and the remaining cup of whole corn kernels. Blend in the cream.

Pour half of the mixture into a buttered baking pan. Sprinkle with half of the Cheddar cheese and chopped chilies. Spread on the rest of the mixture and cover with the rest of the chilies and cheese. Cover the pan with foil and bake at 375° for 1 hour. Cool for 15 minutes before serving. *Serves 6.*

Filling

6 eggs, separated
¾ cup sugar
½ teaspoon almond extract
½ teaspoon vanilla extract
⅓ cup amaretto liqueur
6 ounces unsweetened chocolate
3 ounces semisweet or bittersweet chocolate
½ cup butter
⅓ cup strong liquid coffee
1¼ cups heavy cream, whipped stiff

To make the crust, melt the butter and chocolate together in a double boiler. Stir in the almond extract and the almonds. Let the mixture cool slightly and press into the bottom of a buttered, 10-inch springform pan. Set aside.

Beat the egg yolks with the sugar, flavoring extracts, and amaretto with an electric mixer until thick, about 5 minutes. Cook over a double boiler for about 15 minutes, stirring until very thick and pale yellow. Set aside.

Melt the chocolates together in a double boiler, beat in the butter and add to the egg custard mixture. Whisk in the coffee and let the mixture cool slightly. Fold in the whipped cream.

Beat the egg whites until stiff and fold them into the mixture. Pour into the prepared crust. Smooth the top and tap the pan to remove any air bubbles. Refrigerate until firm; at least 4 hours, overnight is better.

Serve with sweetened whipped cream and Raspberry Sauce (see page 77), if desired. *Serves 16.*

*H*oused in a historical landmark, Metropole is a bastion of French cuisine. The dining rooms of the restaurant provide a faintly medieval European country-inn setting for the three-star training and talents of chef-owner Serge Bled. The menu is devoted to provincial cooking, with an emphasis on seafood and game dishes, some based on recipes dating back to the seventeenth century.

Compliments of

METROPOLE
BERKELEY

Petrale Sole Boisliveau

Fillet of Sole Stuffed
with Spinach and Endive

An invention of Metropole's chef-owner Serge Bled, this is a dish that has its roots in classic French cooking. As its preparation is elaborate and time-consuming, keep the rest of the dinner simple. A French-style risotto (actually a pilaf made with seafood stock) would be a good accompaniment, while a vegetable course could round out the menu.

1 tablespoon butter
1 tablespoon olive oil
½ bunch spinach
2 heads Belgian endive, leaves separated
Salt and pepper
4 medium-sized fresh petrale fillets, about
   1½ pounds total

Poaching Liquid

1 cup dry white wine
1 teaspoon chopped shallot
1 cup fish stock
4 tablespoons melted butter

Sauce

Reserved poaching liquid
1 cup heavy cream
Pinch of saffron
1 leek, white part only, cut in fine julienne
½ carrot, cut in fine julienne
Salt and ground white pepper

Heat the butter and olive oil in a sauté pan or skillet until foaming and cook the spinach and endive separately, about 15 seconds for the spinach and a minute for the endive, seasoning each with salt and pepper to taste. Let them drain and cool, and then cut the endive crosswise into 3 or 4 pieces. Combine the greens.

Lay the sole "skin" side up (the smoother side) on the work surface and split each fillet in half lengthwise. Flatten them slightly with a cleaver, and season with a little salt and pepper. Place the spinach-endive filling on each fillet and roll up, securing with a toothpick.

To make the poaching liquid, stir the wine, shallot, fish stock, and butter together in a shallow nonreactive pan just large enough to hold the fillets in 1 layer. Place the rolled fillets, seam side down, in the mixture. Bring to a boil, cover the pan, and simmer until the sole is just cooked through, about 10 minutes, depending on the size of the fillets (the flesh should just barely be opaque). Gently remove the fillets with a slotted spoon, drain them, and keep them warm while preparing the sauce.

To make the sauce, over high heat, reduce the poaching liquid by one-half. Add the cream and saffron and reduce further, until thick enough to coat the back of a spoon. Add the julienne of leek and carrot, simmer for 30 seconds, season with salt and pepper to taste, and pour immediately over the fish. *Serves 4.*

Boeuf Gribiche

Beef with Gribiche Sauce

Served with a green salad and a good, hearty rye bread, and the broth from the ribs as a first course, this makes a plentiful meal. For use as an appetizer in a larger menu, use only half the recipe.

4 to 5 pounds fairly lean short ribs of beef
Beef stock to cover ribs

Sauce

1 cup mayonnaise
2 tablespoons cornichons, chopped very fine
1 tablespoon capers, drained
2 tablespoons minced chives (fresh, if possible)
2 tablespoons minced fresh parsley
1 shallot, minced
1 garlic clove, minced
3 hard-cooked eggs, minced
2½ tablespoons French red wine vinegar
1½ cups good vegetable oil
2 or 3 drops Tabasco sauce
1½ teaspoons Dijon mustard
2 tablespoons fresh lemon juice
½ teaspoon honey
3 or 4 drops Worcestershire sauce
Pinch of salt and pepper

Place the short ribs and the stock in a deep, heavy pot, bring to a full boil, then cover, lower the heat and simmer until very tender, 1½ to 3 hours. When cooked, cool, bone the ribs and take off most of the fat. The stock can be served as a first course.

To make the sauce, into the mayonnaise mix the cornichons, capers, chives, parsley, shallot, garlic, and eggs. Combine all the remaining ingredients and add to the mayonnaise mixture, blending well; chill. (The sauce and meat may be kept refrigerated for 4 to 5 days.)

Before serving, slice the meat into long slices, cutting in the direction the bone ran. Put the meat in a saucepan with some of the stock, bring to a boil, cover, and simmer 3 to 5 minutes, or until the meat is heated through. It must be served very, very hot, as the sauce is to be served cold over it. This sauce also goes well with white fish. *Serves 8 to 10.*

Chives

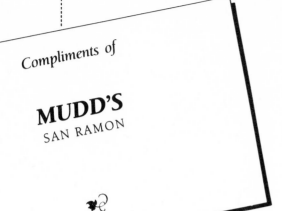

Compliments of

MUDD'S
SAN RAMON

The fare at Mudd's Restaurant is hearty seasonal American cuisine with specialties featuring produce, herbs, and flowers from the surrounding gardens. The restaurant is simple yet elegant, and all the dining areas overlook the gardens, that were started two years before the restaurant opened in 1981. Mudd's also offers a wide range of food and gardening classes, a summer food and concert series, and a summer nature camp for children.

Root Vegetable Soup

A hearty winter soup to warm your soul.

1 onion
2 pinches thyme
1 bay leaf
Olive oil
1 cup white wine
1 quart chicken stock
1 celery root, coarsely chopped
3 white potatoes, coarsely chopped
1 small turnip, coarsely chopped
¼ baguette, thinly sliced
Salt and pepper

Sauté the onion, thyme, and bay leaf in a little olive oil. Add the white wine and boil for 1 or 2 minutes to remove the alcohol. Add the chicken stock and the other vegetables and bring to a boil. Simmer for 30 to 40 minutes, until the celery root is soft. Sauté the bread slices in olive oil until golden brown. Purée the soup and the croutons in a blender. Adjust the thickness with milk and season with salt and pepper. *Serves 6.*

Apple Crisp

The American classic dessert, apple crisp, depends on the use of really tart and flavorful apples. The Mudd's version adds nuts to the traditional crumb topping. Any combination of nuts you prefer can be used.

12 large tart cooking apples
1 teaspoon cinnamon
¼ teaspoon nutmeg
¼ cup white sugar
⅔ cup walnuts, chopped
⅔ cup pecans, chopped
⅔ cup almonds, chopped
1 cup brown sugar
1 cup flour
½ pound unsalted butter, chilled and diced

Peel, core, and slice the apples. Mix them with cinnamon, nutmeg, and white sugar and bake them, covered, in a 9- or 10-inch nonreactive pie pan at 350° for 20 minutes.

Toast the nuts at 300° for 10 minutes. When cool, chop them in a food processor until they are the size of very coarse bread crumbs. Mix the remaining ingredients together, top the baked apple slices, and bake for another 30 minutes, until the topping is brown. Serve with whipped cream. *Serves 8.*

Garden Lasagna

This lasagna, packed with vegetables from the garden, makes a lovely departure from the usual noodle and cheese dish. Make sure your tomato sauce is very well seasoned with garlic and fresh herbs to get the full flavor of this recipe.

2 medium zucchini
2 medium yellow summer squash
1 cup chopped and diced green cabbage
1 small green bell pepper
1 small red bell pepper
8 ounces low-fat mozzarella cheese
2 cups ricotta cheese
2 ounces grated Parmesan cheese
½ cup plus 2 tablespoons chopped fresh
   herbs: basil, oregano, marjoram, and parsley
4 cloves garlic
Salt and pepper
2 sheets fresh spinach pasta, each 8 by 12
   inches
3 to 4 cups tomato sauce
6 ounces grated Jack cheese

Cut all the vegetables in small dice and mix with the mozzarella, ricotta, and Parmesan cheeses, ½ cup herbs, garlic, and salt and pepper to taste.

The pasta is cooked in whole sheets, so you will need a large pot of rapidly boiling salted water, a large colander, and another large pot, or sink, of cold water. Cook the pasta for 1 minute only; it will finish cooking in the casserole. Tip the contents of the large pot gently into the colander; the pasta will break if you try to remove the whole sheet. Then slide the pasta into the cold water to stop the cooking. With both hands, gently remove the pasta, spread the sheets out flat on a towel, and blot them dry.

Lay one sheet out flat and spread it with half the vegetable and cheese mixture. Lay the second sheet of pasta over it and top with the remaining mixture. Fold the lasagna in half lengthwise and trim off the unfilled pasta from the ends.

Place the lasagna in a baking dish, cover with the tomato sauce, top with grated Jack cheese, sprinkle with the remaining minced fresh herbs, and bake in a 350° oven until heated through, about 30 to 45 minutes.
Serves 6.

This restaurant is sought out by loyal patrons for its conservative European atmosphere and traditional Continental dinners. Lunches, by contrast, feature a more current California style. Housed in a two-story frame house that was originally the site for the legendary Pot Luck Restaurant, the interior features an enormous central skylight.

Compliments of

NADINE RESTAURANT
BERKELEY

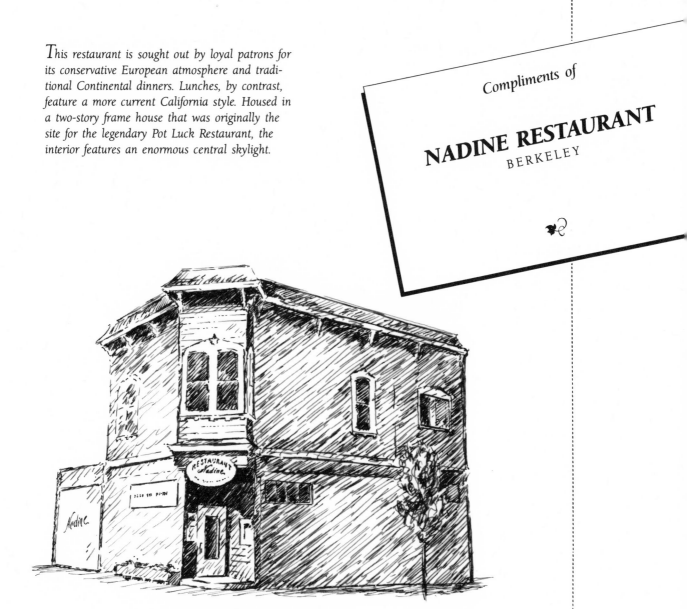

Spring Chicken Salad

This makes a gorgeous sight: a fan of endive leaves and snow peas accented by red tomatoes, with white shreds of chicken breast in the center. An easy dish to make, it will accommodate many vegetables other than the ones listed.

½ cup sesame seeds
2 whole chicken breasts, halved, skinned, and
　boned
Salt and pepper
4 shallots, minced
3 garlic cloves, minced
1 tablespoon Dijon mustard
1 egg
¼ cup Oriental sesame oil
1½ cups olive oil or other vegetable oil
½ cup red wine vinegar
Grated zest of 1 orange
½ pound snow peas
2 tomatoes, sliced
2 Belgian endives
2 green onions

Toast the sesame seeds for 2 to 3 minutes in a 300° oven. Remove and increase the oven temperature to 375°. Place the chicken on a buttered pan, sprinkle with salt and pepper, cover with waxed paper, and bake for about 15 minutes or until the breasts are springy to the touch, not mushy or unyielding. Allow the chicken to cool, then slice lengthwise into ½-inch strips.

Blend the shallots, garlic, mustard, and egg in a blender or food processor or with a hand whisk. Slowly add the oils to the mixture while puréeing or whisking. Slowly add the red wine vinegar. Add the orange zest and toasted sesame seeds.

Blanch the snow peas by dipping them in boiling water for 2 minutes; immediately plunge them into cold water. Arrange the snow peas, tomatoes, endives, and green onions on a platter. Place the chicken in a mound in the center. Pour half of the dressing over the arrangement and serve, passing the remainder on the side. *Serves 4.*

Sautéed Sole with Hazelnut-Butter Sauce

The hazelnut-butter sauce can be made an hour before serving (see Basics on beurre blanc), making the production of this dish very simple indeed. Petrale sole, flounder, or eastern sole is preferred.

½ cup hazelnuts
¼ cup minced shallots
2 tablespoons minced garlic
1 cup dry white wine
2 tablespoons fresh lemon juice
1 cup (2 sticks) unsalted butter, cut into small pieces
2 eggs
¾ cup half and half
2 pounds sole fillets
Flour
1 tablespoon olive oil or other vegetable oil
1 tablespoon butter

Toast the hazelnuts in a 300° oven for 7 minutes. Allow them to cool, then mince. A food processor is ideal for this. Combine the shallots, garlic, wine, and lemon juice in a small nonreactive saucepan and reduce to one-third. Slowly whisk in the butter a bit at a time. Add the hazelnuts and remove the pan to a warm place.

Mix the eggs and half and half together. Dredge the sole in the flour, shake off the excess, and dip the fillets in the egg batter. Heat the oil and butter. When the butter foams but before it browns, add the fish and sauté for 2 to 3 minutes on the first side and 1 to 2 minutes on the second side. Serve immediately, with the sauce on the side or poured over the fish. *Serves 6.*

Compliments of

NAKAPAN
BERKELEY

The most elegant entry into Berkeley's ever-growing group of ethnic restaurants, Nakapan is the offspring of a Bangkok restaurant. After ten years there, owner Orrawan Chaloeicheep came to this country and selected a surprising site for his elegant Thai cuisine: a building with an imaginatively contoured split-level redwood interior. The contrast of exotic foods in a contemporary California setting works surprisingly well; the Bangkok cuisine itself is authentic down to the specially imported covered bowls in which the soup is served. Not all the dishes are as hot as one might expect, and the menu is divided into sections of hot and mild dishes.

Barbecued Chicken with Cabbage Salad

Picnic fare at its best. The cool but spicy cabbage salad balances the chicken to perfection.

9 garlic cloves, minced
Three 1-inch pieces fresh ginger, minced
1½ teaspoons ground black pepper
1½ teaspoons salt
2 teaspoons chopped fresh cilantro
1 tablespoon chopped coriander (cilantro)
  root or stems
1½ tablespoons soy sauce
1 teaspoon ground caraway
1 whole chicken, cut into quarters
3 tablespoons vegetable oil
Cabbage Salad, following

Mix together the garlic, ginger, pepper, salt, cilantro, coriander root or stems, soy sauce, and caraway. Mix with the chicken pieces. Sprinkle the oil over all. Marinate at least 4 hours or overnight. Cook over charcoal until the juices run clear when the thigh of the chicken is pierced with a knife, about 30 minutes. Serve with cabbage salad. *Serves 4.*

Cabbage Salad

4 cups shredded cabbage
2 cups shredded carrots
5 tablespoons fresh lime juice
1 garlic clove, minced
1 teaspoon sugar
Fish sauce or salt to taste
1 to 2 teaspoons dried red pepper flakes

Mix the cabbage and carrots. Mix the lime juice, garlic, sugar and fish sauce or salt together, and pour over the cabbage and carrots. Sprinkle the red pepper flakes on top. *Serves 4.*

Red Snapper à la Bangkok

This recipe demonstrates the Chinese influences on Thai cooking. The mild and complex sauce blends subtly with the citrus fragrances of the steamed fish. If red snapper is unavailable, any firm, white-fleshed fish may be substituted. The pickled plums are available in Chinese markets.

1 ounce dried black mushrooms
1 cup warm water
2 tablespoons vegetable oil
1 garlic clove, minced
1-inch piece fresh ginger, minced
4 Chinese pickled plums, seeded, and
  chopped
1 teaspoon sugar
2 tablespoons oyster sauce
¾ teaspoon ground white pepper
1 tablespoon soy sauce
½ cup sliced fresh lemon grass
3 dried lime leaves
2 pounds red snapper fillets
4 green onions, sliced thin

Soak the mushrooms in the warm water for 30 minutes. Drain the mushrooms, reserving the mushroom water. Cut the mushrooms into slices. Heat the oil in a saucepan over medium heat. Sauté the garlic until it is light brown. Add the mushrooms, ginger, plums, sugar, oyster sauce, white pepper, and soy sauce. Simmer for 5 minutes, adding the reserved mushroom water if the sauce becomes too thick or threatens to scorch.

While the sauce simmers, steam the fish: Place half the lemon grass and 1 lime leaf in the bottom of a steamer basket; add the fish and top with the rest of the lemon grass and lime leaves. Steam for about 5 minutes, depending on the thickness of the fish (it should be very slightly translucent in the center). To finish the sauce, add the rest of the mushroom soaking water and the green onions and bring to a boil. If the sauce is still too thick, use water from the steamer to thin it. Serve the sauce over the fish. *Serves 6.*

----------------------- ❦ -----------------------

Green Curry Beef

Another dish from Thailand and, as one might expect, a spicy one. The recipe provides for a milder version.

3½ cups unsweetened coconut milk
Green Curry Paste, following
3 pounds aged top sirloin steak, cut into
   1-inch cubes
4 tablespoons fish sauce
½ teaspoon sugar
3 dried lemon leaves
2 cups fresh or frozen green peas
4 green chilies, cut lengthwise into narrow
   strips (*serrano* or *jalapeño* chilies are hot;
   for a milder version, use 1 green bell
   pepper)
2 tablespoons chopped basil
Whole basil leaves

In a saucepan, heat 1 cup of the coconut milk, stirring constantly until it comes to a boil. Lower the heat and continue cooking, stirring occasionally, until the coconut milk thickens and oil bubbles around it. By this time it should be reduced to one quarter of the original amount.

Add the green curry paste and fry for 5 minutes, stirring constantly. The curry paste will smell cooked and the oil will separate from it when it is ready. Add the beef and cook over medium heat, stirring frequently and turning the pieces until they are cooked to your taste, about 3 minutes for medium rare. Add the remaining coconut milk and the fish sauce, sugar, and lemon leaves. Bring to a boil, stirring. Add the peas, green chilies, and basil. Stir briefly. Remove from heat. Serve with steamed rice and decorate with basil leaves. *Serves 6 to 8.*

Green Curry Paste

2 tablespoons peanut oil
10 *serrano* chilies or 2 green
   bell peppers, cut up
2 tablespoons chopped fresh lemon grass and
   lemon peel, mixed
1 teaspoon chopped fresh cilantro
1 tablespoon chopped red onion
7 whole white peppercorns
1 teaspoon salt
2 garlic cloves

Heat the oil in a wok or a skillet and stir-fry the remaining ingredients until the chilies are soft. Pound with a mortar until a smooth paste or use a blender or food processor, adding a little water to ease the grinding.

Phillip Chu, the owner and chef, is proud of what he calls "the first full Burmese dinner menu outside of Burma." Situated south of China and east of India, the Burmese draw from both neighbors to create a unique cooking style. The menu at Nan Yang is based on Burmese home cooking and the dishes served in food stalls.

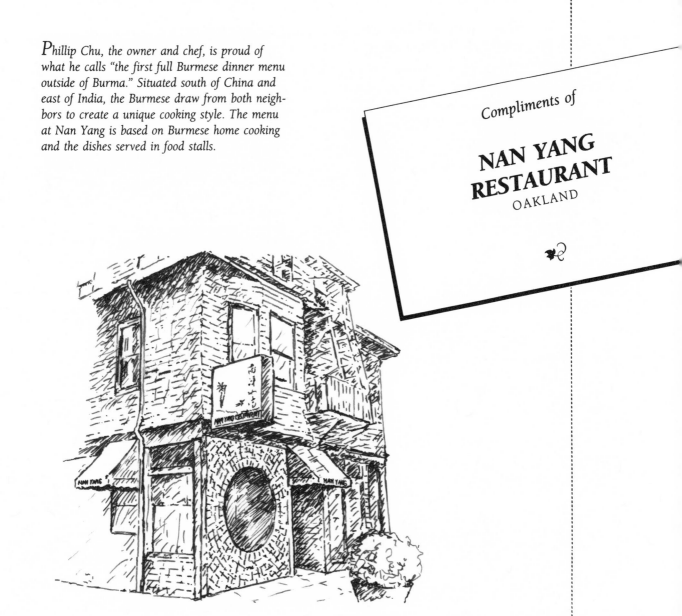

Compliments of

NAN YANG RESTAURANT
OAKLAND

Burmese Curried Beef Stew

*T*his dish, and the one that follows, are unusual even for curry. The handling of the ingredients is simple, but the resulting flavors are complex. In both dishes, care must be taken to achieve the right moisture content. Also, both dishes call for curry powder; it is worth the trouble to go to a specialty grocer to get a top-quality powder.

This curry combines the sweetness of cinnamon with the tartness of tamarind. It is a bit hot and may be made hotter if you like it that way. The beef does tend to dry out while cooking and may need the addition of more water to keep the sauce at the right consistency.

1 pound boneless beef chuck
4 tablespoons oil
3 cloves garlic, chopped
1 stalk lemon grass
1 teaspoon tamarind powder
1 stick cinnamon, 2 inches long
2 tablespoons minced fresh ginger
2 tablespoons curry powder
¼ teaspoon chili powder
¾ tablespoon salt
¼ teaspoon cayenne, more or less, to taste
4 to 6 cups water
2 medium potatoes, peeled
Cilantro sprigs for garnish

Cut the beef in 1½-inch cubes and sear in oil for a few minutes. Lower the heat, add the garlic, lemon grass, tamarind, cinnamon, ginger, curry powder, chili powder, salt, and cayenne, and cook for another couple of minutes. Add the water and simmer, covered, for about an hour.

Add the potatoes and continue cooking until the beef is very tender and the potatoes are done. The potatoes should have disintegrated somewhat, contributing to the thickness of the sauce. If the curry seems too thick during cooking, add another cup of water.

When the meat is tender, skim off the excess fat and serve, garnished with cilantro. *Serves 4.*

Curried Spinach and Tomatoes

Another dish that repays attention. The spinach tends to be watery and will lose its bright color if cooked too long.

1 bunch spinach
1½ tablespoons vegetable or peanut oil
1 medium onion, minced
1 teaspoon curry powder
2 cloves garlic
2 tomatoes, coarsely chopped
Half a Thai chili, sliced across
1½ tablespoons rice vinegar
½ teaspoon salt

Wash the spinach, cut off the roots, and cut the leaves, still on the stems, into thirds.

Heat the oil and stir-fry the onion for a minute, until it begins to soften. Add the curry powder and cook for another minute, taking care not to burn it. Add the garlic, tomatoes, chili, salt, and rice vinegar and cook for another minute or two, until the tomatoes begin to give off their moisture. Add the spinach and cook for another few minutes, until the spinach is done to your liking. *Serves 4.*

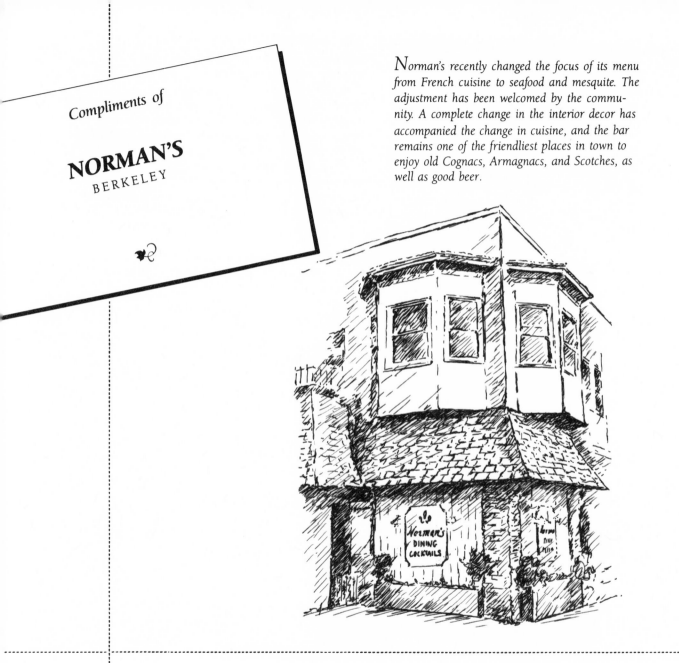

Compliments of

NORMAN'S
BERKELEY

Norman's recently changed the focus of its menu from French cuisine to seafood and mesquite. The adjustment has been welcomed by the community. A complete change in the interior decor has accompanied the change in cuisine, and the bar remains one of the friendliest places in town to enjoy old Cognacs, Armagnacs, and Scotches, as well as good beer.

Poached Salmon with Beurre Rosé and Golden Caviar

Use only the best-quality salmon, halibut, or sea bass, and a good-quality dry rosé wine, to make this lavish dish. Beurre rosé is a variation of beurre blanc, page 19.

Beurre Rosé

2 cups dry rosé wine
½ teaspoon minced shallot
¼ cup fresh lemon juice
Pinch of dried herbs of your choice, or
   1 teaspoon minced fresh herbs (fresh
   marjoram or oregano works well)
1 cup (2 sticks) unsalted butter, cut into
   pieces

Court Bouillon

1 small onion
1 small carrot
1 celery stalk
10 whole black peppercorns
1 small lemon, cut in quarters
¼ cup red wine vinegar
About 1 quart cold water

Six 6-ounce salmon fillets
1 ounce golden caviar

To make the *beurre rosé*, in a small, heavy saucepan, reduce the wine, shallot, lemon juice, and dried herbs to ¼ cup. Whisk in the butter bit by bit over low heat. Set the sauce aside and keep it warm. If you are using fresh herbs, they should be added just before serving.

Simmer the court bouillon ingredients in a nonreactive pot for 20 minutes, then strain. Reserve the liquid and discard the vegetables. Bring the court bouillon to a boil in a shallow nonreactive pan, reduce the heat to a simmer, and poach the fish for about 7 minutes. Remove the fillets with a slotted spoon, drain, and serve immediately, topped with the sauce and a small spoonful of caviar. *Serves 6.*

Steamed Sole with Papaya

A hallmark of California cooking is the simple preparation of absolutely fresh ingredients. This dish requires the most impeccable petrale sole, and papaya at the peak of ripeness.

2 pounds petrale sole fillets, split lengthwise
Salt and ground white pepper to taste
6 spinach leaves, or 1 spinach leaf for each
   piece of fish
1 large ripe papaya
1 small garlic clove, minced
1 small slice fresh ginger, minced
Tabasco to taste
Lemon juice to taste
8 to 16 cilantro leaves

Place the fillets "skin" side down (the smoother side). Salt and pepper the fillets and place a spinach leaf on each. Peel and seed the papaya and cut into quarters. Split one quarter lengthwise and cut the resulting eighths into as many pieces as you have fish. Use more papaya if necessary. Place a piece of papaya on each spinach leaf and roll the fillet jelly-roll fashion from the tail end. Secure with a toothpick.

Purée the remaining papaya with the garlic, ginger, Tabasco, and lemon juice in a blender or food processor. Season with salt and pepper to taste.

In a steamer, steam the fish rolls for about 3 minutes, depending on the size of the fillets. Serve with the papaya purée poured over, and garnish with cilantro. *Serves 6.*

Maggie Klein, a writer about food, and Bob Klein, a T.V. executive, have realized a fond dream with this bustling, street-level café and elegant upstairs restaurant, in the heart of Oakland's exciting new open market complex. Oliveto's chef, Rick Hackett, focuses on rustic European cuisine with simple, succulent fare based on fresh herbs, garlic, peppers, and olive oil. Meats and produce fresh from the farm are mainstays at Oliveto.

Inspired by the theme of her cookbook, The Feast of the Olive (Aris, 1983), and with the help of husband Rob and the talented kitchen staff, Maggie has brought the tastes of Tuscany and the Mediterranean to the upstairs dining room, and delicious pizzas and tapas-style little dishes to the Café.

Compliments of

OLIVETO CAFÉ AND RESTAURANT
BERKELEY

Braised Lamb Shanks with Fresh Shellbeans, Tomato, and Herbs

Here is the kind of comfortable, rustic dish we all thrive on. Lamb shank is a wonderful meat for braising. After two or three hours of cooking, it nearly falls from the bone, but because of its high gelatin content, it remains juicy and succulent. The recipe calls for fresh cranberry beans, but any kind of fresh shelling bean or pea will work. (A fresh shellbean is simply any bean that is harvested when fully formed, but not dry. Dry beans can certainly be used, but they must be added at the beginning of the cooking and you must add a cup of stock.)

4 lamb shanks, trimmed of silverskin and fat
2 tablespoons olive oil
1 onion, diced
3 cloves garlic, minced
1 cup white wine
6 tomatoes, roasted in a 350° oven for 30 minutes, peeled, and puréed
1 tablespoon chopped oregano or marjoram
¼ cup Italian parsley
1 tablespoon chopped rosemary
1 cup fresh cranberry beans
1 teaspoon salt
½ teaspoon pepper, freshly ground

In a heavy, nonreactive casserole, sear the meat in the olive oil. Remove it to a plate. If the oil has burned, pour it out and add a tablespoon of fresh oil. Reduce the heat, add the onion and garlic, and cook until transparent. Deglaze the pan with the wine, then add the tomatoes, herbs, and lamb shanks.

If you are using dry instead of fresh beans, add them at this point, along with 1 cup of stock. Bring to a simmer, cover and bake in a 300° oven for 1½ hours.

If you are using fresh beans, add them after the first ½ hour and cook until the lamb and beans are tender, about another 1 to 1½ hours.

Skim off the excess grease and adjust the seasoning with salt and freshly ground pepper. *Serves 2 to 4, depending on the size of the lamb shanks.*

Risotto with Smoked Chicken, Artichoke, and Parmigiano

Risotto *is a Northern Italian dish traditionally made with a short-grain hard rice which, when cooked slowly, with gradual additions of liquid, becomes a rich soul-warming first or second course, or the basis of a simple meal. Arborio rice from Italy is perfect for* risotto *because it's starchy quality makes for a very creamy texture.*

4 to 6 cups chicken stock
2 tablespoons olive oil
1½ cups Arborio rice (available at Italian groceries or specialty stores)
1 small onion, finely diced
1 carrot, finely diced
1 rib celery, finely diced
6 fresh artichoke hearts, or 1 package frozen artichoke hearts
½ to ¾ cup white wine
Salt to taste
6 ounces smoked chicken
3 tablespoons sweet butter
½ cup Parmigiano-Reggiano cheese, grated
3 tablespoons minced Italian parsley

Bring the chicken stock to a boil and reduce to a simmer.

Coat a saucepan with olive oil and add the rice. Cook for 1 to 2 minutes, until the rice becomes translucent. Add the onion, carrot, celery, artichokes, and wine and salt to taste.

Add 6 to 8 ounces of chicken stock at a time, cook, stirring constantly, until the liquid is absorbed. Continue the process until the rice is just *al dente*, about 15 to 20 minutes from the time you first added the stock.

Once the rice is tender and creamy, but still *al dente*, add the smoked chicken, butter, and cheese. Cover and let rest for 2 minutes. Stir in the parsley and serve. *Serves 4 to 6.*

Compliments of

OMNIVORE
BERKELEY

Founded in 1977, Omnivore was sold in 1984 by our coauthor, chef Paul Johnston. Based on the principle that people are omnivorous creatures, and the preference of the chef not to confine himself to any single style of cuisine, the restaurant has always lived up to its name. The new owner, Andy Lee, carries on that tradition. Despite the miniscule kitchen, which greets diners as they enter, the food is of consistently high quality. The original recipes and cooking staff remain, and the focus on high-quality ingredients and inventiveness continues.

Mushroom and Pecan Pâté

Since the recipe for this rich and savory vegetarian loaf is quite large, chill the leftover pâté and serve it sliced as an appetizer or in sandwiches with a pungent mustard and cornichons. Another variation is to convert this into a sausage recipe: Roll the pâté mixture in plastic wrap, poach, and serve with the sauce. This dish is an extraordinary treat during wild mushroom season, and was originally designed for chanterelles.

The sauce is related to beurre blanc; refer to the Basics section for more information.

6 cups chopped mushrooms (a mixture of domestic, chanterelles, and dried mushrooms)
1 cup hot water
1 onion, minced
½ cup butter
½ teaspoon salt
1 thyme sprig, chopped
8 eggs, lightly beaten
1 cup shredded Swiss cheese (Emmenthaler)
1 cup ground pecans

Sauce

Reserved mushroom-soaking liquid
Reserved mushroom-cooking liquid
3 tablespoons fresh lemon juice
¼ cup dry sherry, Madeira, or dry white wine
1 cup heavy cream
1 cup unsalted butter, chilled

Soak the dried mushrooms in the hot water for 30 minutes. Drain, reserving the soaking liquid for the sauce. Discard any tough stems. In a heavy sauté pan or skillet, cook the onion in the butter over low heat until the onion is soft. Add the mushrooms, salt, and thyme. Cover, raise the heat, and cook for 10 minutes, stirring several times. Remove from the heat, transfer the mushroom mixture to a strainer, and press out as much of the liquid as possible. Reserve the liquid for the sauce. Allow the mushrooms to cool. Mix them with the eggs, cheese, and pecans. Add additional salt to taste. Pack into a buttered 9-by-3-inch loaf pan and cover with foil. Place the loaf pan in a larger pan containing boiling water. The water bath should come halfway up the side of the loaf pan. Bake in a preheated 325° oven for 1 hour, or until the pâté is firm and slightly puffed. Allow to set for 20 minutes.

Meanwhile, prepare the sauce: Place the mushroom liquids, lemon juice, wine, and cream into a heavy, nonreactive pan. Reduce over low heat until syrupy, with only 6 or 7 tablespoons remaining. Cut the cold butter into 8 pieces. Over the low heat, stirring constantly, add 1 piece of butter at a time to the liquid mixture. If the sauce seems too tart, add more butter or cream. Unmold the pâté and serve with the sauce poured over. The pâté may also be served cold. *Serves 8 to 10.*

Green Seafood Soup

A hearty main-course soup meant to take advantage of fresh herbs in season. With the exception of the dried thyme used in the first part of the recipe, dried herbs are not appropriate. The herbs and their proportions are only suggestions. Let availability determine your final choices.

Potato-Fumet Purée

1 medium onion
4 tablespoons butter
2 whole garlic cloves
1 medium potato, diced
1 cup dry white wine
1 thyme sprig, or ½ teaspoon dried thyme
4 cups fish stock

Green Purée

1 bunch spinach
1 cup fish stock
1 bunch sorrel
1 bunch watercress
1 bunch rocket (arugula)
Leaves from 4 oregano sprigs
Leaves from 2 tarragon sprigs
1 bunch fresh chives or green onions

1 cup heavy cream or half and half
4 ounces each rockfish, angler, salmon, halibut
  or sea bass, and sole (totaling 20 ounces),
  cut in finger-sized pieces
Salt and ground black pepper to taste
Drops of lemon juice to taste
Small handful of chopped fresh herbs (chives,
  rocket, parsley, tarragon, etc.)

In a nonreactive saucepan, gently sauté the onion in the butter until it is soft but not colored. Add the garlic and diced potato and stir for a moment. Add the wine and raise the heat, cooking until the alcohol has evaporated. Add the thyme and fish stock. Simmer until the potatoes are tender, about 20 minutes. Remove the herb stem and purée the mixture in a blender or food processor. Set aside.

Roughly chop the spinach, after making sure it is clean and free of grit (it usually takes 3 immersions in water in a large container or sink; the sand will settle to the bottom). Pack the spinach into the bottom of a blender or food processor and begin to purée, adding fish stock as necessary to keep things moving. As the spinach purées, add the other greens, herbs, and onions until they are all incorporated. Set the mixture aside.

Combine the potato-fumet purée and the green purée with the cream and bring to a simmer. Add the rockfish and angler and simmer for 2 or 3 minutes. Add the salmon and halibut or sea bass, simmer for another 2 or 3 minutes, then add the sole, simmering for another 2 to 3 minutes, until all the fish is done. Season with salt, pepper, and lemon juice. Garnish with the chopped herbs and serve immediately. *Serves 4.*

NOTE: This dish can be made with only one or two different kinds of fish, totaling 20 ounces, but a variety of fish will make a better soup.

COMPLIMENTS OF THE CHEF

Suprêmes de Volaille Parmesan

Boneless Chicken Breasts with Parmesan Cheese

This is an addictive dish; the lemony sauce, crisp cheese coating, and juicy chicken are elementally satisfying. The recipe is simple, with three caveats: Avoid overcooking (a dry chicken breast is a dreadful thing); be sure the butter for the sauce is cold; use the highest heat your stove can produce to cook the sauce.

3 whole chicken breasts, skinned, boned, and halved
2 eggs, beaten
½ cup bread crumbs
½ cup freshly grated Parmesan cheese
2 tablespoons peanut or olive oil

Sauce

¾ cup cold salted butter (1½ sticks)
6 tablespoons fresh lemon juice
Splash of white wine (optional)
Handful of parsley sprigs, chopped

Trim the *suprêmes* of fat and the largest tendons. Combine the eggs and suprêmes in a mixing bowl, making sure the chicken is thoroughly coated. Mix the crumbs and cheese together in a flat, shallow pan. With your left hand, remove 1 chicken breast, place in the breading mixture, and press the crumbs and cheese in well. Transfer the chicken to another pan and sprinkle a bit of breading over. Repeat with each breast, reserving your left hand for the wet egg mixture, keeping the right hand dry. Distribute leftover breading among the breasts. Refrigerate for 1 to 4 hours or overnight.

Heat the oil in a large sauté pan or skillet. A well-seasoned cast-iron skillet works best for this. Avoid stainless steel and ceramic surfaces; the chicken will stick. Cook for about 5 to 7 minutes, then turn and cook another 3 minutes, until the breasts are springy, not mushy to the touch. If they feel quite solid, they are overdone. Remove to heated plates.

To make the sauce, pour the oil out of the chicken cooking pan, or use a small clean saucepan. Cook the butter, lemon juice, and wine over high heat until all the butter is melted and a foamy sauce forms. If the sauce begins to look oily and separated, add a splash of wine. Add the parsley. Pour over the chicken and serve with boiled new potatoes and a simple steamed vegetable. *Serves 6.*

NOTE: The sauce may be varied by the addition of fresh herbs, garlic, capers, chilies, green onions, minced tomatoes, fresh ginger, soy sauce, or lime juice instead of lemon juice, etc.

Fish with Wild Mushroom-Cream Sauce

A rich entrée worthy of the best fish available, especially if wild mushrooms are in season. The basic concept can be adapted to fowl or veal by using the appropriate stock in the sauce and substituting sherry or Madeira for the white wine. We tested the recipe with salmon, to everyone's delight.

2 tablespoons minced shallots
6 tablespoons butter
8 ounces wild mushrooms (chanterelles are especially good), or 8 ounces domestic mushrooms plus 1 ounce dried wild mushrooms (*cèpes, porcini,* or *shiitake*)
1 teaspoon flour
2 cups boiling fish stock
¼ cup dry white wine
1 thyme sprig, or ½ teaspoon dried thyme
2 cups heavy cream
Flour
Six 5- to 6-ounce fish fillets (salmon, sea bass, halibut, or rockfish)
2 tablespoons brandy
Drops of lemon juice
Salt

In a large, heavy saucepan, cook the shallots slowly in 4 tablespoons of the butter. Raise the heat and add the mushrooms, cooking until their water is evaporated and the pan is dry. (Wild mushrooms usually give off large amounts of water. If using dried mushrooms, soak in hot water to cover for 1 hour before cooking.) Sprinkle the flour over the mushrooms in the pan, mix well, and cook for about 3 minutes. Add the boiling stock, wine, and thyme and cook 5 minutes. Add the cream and reduce to the desired consistency.

Lightly flour the fish and sauté it in the remaining 2 tablespoons of butter. Remove the fish to a warm platter. Flame the pan with the brandy. Transfer the sauce to the fish sauté pan, season to taste with lemon juice and salt, and serve the sauce poured over the fish. *Serves 6.*

Panini offers fast, delicious sandwiches in the heart of downtown Berkeley. However, when Lee Ann Sandefer, chef and co-owner with Jeffrey Masson, says that Panini's sandwich offerings are "slightly untraditional," that is something of an understatement. How often have you ordered a tuna sandwich and been served freshly poached tuna? Not only are you sure to have an exceptional sandwich here, but Panini's off-street location offers a secluded outdoor seating area in which to enjoy it. And, if you are lucky enough to live near Kensington in the East Bay, you can buy your bread from Semifreddi's Bakery, just as Panini does.

The recipes that follow are simply called sandwiches. Actually, they are complex structures of ingredients and flavors, and should not be undertaken as lightly as, say, a ham and swiss on rye. They are built up using many components and the result is rewarding.

Compliments of

PANINI
BERKELEY

Smoked Chicken and Avocado Sandwich with Ginger-Sesame Mayonnaise

This recipe makes just over a cup and a half of mayonnaise, so you have the opportunity to use the remaining cup as a dip for raw vegetables or artichokes or with grilled fish or chicken.

Ginger-Sesame Mayonnaise

3 egg yolks
⅓ cup dark sesame oil
2 tablespoons soy sauce
1 cup light olive oil
Juice of 1 lemon or lime, or more, to taste
1 large finger (½ inch by 1 inch) fresh ginger, peeled and grated or pulverized in a food processor
2 cloves garlic, mashed

Sandwich

4 *panini* (crusty seeded rolls made from baguette dough) or 1 baguette
1 quarter avocado
4 ounces boneless smoked chicken
1 bunch spinach leaves, washed and stemmed
1 tablespoon scallion, sliced on the diagonal
Sprigs of cilantro
½ teaspoon toasted sesame seeds

To make the mayonnaise, whisk the egg yolks until they thicken a little and lighten in color, then add the sesame oil, drop by drop. As the emulsion forms, add the soy sauce, then slowly add the olive oil, whisking all the time. Next add the lemon or lime juice and the ginger and garlic. The mayonnaise should be fairly tart, so add more citrus juice if needed. *Makes 1½ cups.*

To assemble the sandwich, split the panino or a crusty French roll in half and scoop out some of the center. Spread both sides generously with the Sesame-Ginger Mayonnaise, make a layer of avocado slices, followed by the smoked chicken, spinach leaves, scallion, cilantro, and a sprinkling of sesame seeds. *Makes 4 sandwiches.*

Poached Salmon and Shallot–Cream Cheese Sandwich

Shallot–Cream Cheese

4 ounces cream cheese, at room temperature
4 shallots, finely minced
Zest of 1 lemon, finely grated
Squeeze of lemon juice
Salt and pepper to taste

Poached Salmon

1 cup white wine
1 cup water
Half a carrot, sliced
Half an onion, sliced
1 bay leaf
6 peppercorns
Salt to taste
1 pound whole salmon fillet

Lemon Vinaigrette

1 tablespoon minced shallot
½ teaspoon finely grated lemon zest
Juice of half a lemon
⅓ cup olive oil
Salt and pepper to taste

Sandwich

6 *panini* or 1½ baguettes
Salmon, flaked
Shallot–Cream Cheese spread
Lemon Vinaigrette dressing
Butter lettuce
Fresh basil

Garnish

Butter lettuce
Fresh basil

To make the Shallot–Cream Cheese, combine the cream cheese, shallots, and lemon zest and juice. Add salt and pepper to taste and work until the mixture is easy to spread. The flavor will improve over the course of several hours.

To poach the salmon, make a court bouillon of the wine, water, carrot, onion, bay leaf, and peppercorns, adding salt to taste. Bring the mixture to a boil, reduce the heat, and simmer for 15 minutes.

Strain the bouillon and then poach the salmon in it for 5 to 10 minutes, or until the fish is just done.

Let the salmon cool and then flake it into small pieces.

Make the Lemon Vinaigrette by whisking together the 1 tablespoon minced shallots, ½ teaspoon lemon zest, and juice of half a lemon with the olive oil and adding salt to taste.

Dress the butter lettuce and the salmon, separately, with the Lemon Vinaigrette.

To assemble the sandwich, split a panino or a crusty French roll in half and scoop out some of the center. Generously spread both sides of the roll with the cream cheese mixture. Layer on the butter lettuce and the salmon. Top generously with finely shredded basil. *Makes 6 sandwiches.*

Roast Lamb and Spinach Sandwich with Aioli and Mint Salsa

Mint Salsa

2 large tomatoes, peeled and chopped
Half a white onion, chopped
3 sprigs mint, chopped
3 *jalapeño* chilies, chopped
Juice of half a lemon
1 bunch basil, chopped
¼ cup olive oil

Aioli

1½ cups olive oil
2 large egg yolks
Juice of half a lemon
Salt
White pepper
3 cloves garlic, squeezed through a press or
    pounded in a mortar and pestle

Sandwich

12 slices roasted leg of lamb
6 *panini* or 1½ baguettes
1 bunch spinach, washed and stemmed
Vinaigrette
1 red onion, optional

Make the Mint Salsa by combining the tomatoes, onion, mint, chilies, lemon juice, basil, and olive oil. Set aside.

Then make the Aioli. Whisk the oil into the egg yolks, drop by drop, until the emulsion stiffens. This will use up about half the oil. Add the lemon juice, salt and pepper to taste, and the puréed garlic. Then whisk in the remaining oil slowly.

To assemble the sandwich, cut a panino, crusty French roll, or baguette in half, lengthwise, and scoop out part of the insides. Spread Aioli on both sides, layer spinach dressed lightly with vinaigrette, then a generous covering of mint salsa, and several layers of lamb. Top with red onion, if desired. *Makes 6 sandwiches.*

This high-toned Italian grocery is located in the bustling Rockridge Market Hall. Owners Sara Wilson Houghton and Anthony and Peter Wilson provide over one hundred Bay Area restaurants with such exotic flavors of pasta as garlic, red pepper, and beet. The store also features sausages, pâtés, salads, and cheeses. Under the direction of the chef, Scott Miller, a variety of smoked meats and charcuterie is made on the premises.

Compliments of

PASTA SHOP
OAKLAND

Mushroom Risotto

A basic *risotto recipe that should stand you in good stead, as it accepts variation with ease. Serve risotto immediately; it becomes gummy if kept hot and does not reheat successfully. The quantity of stock given is approximate. It is important to adjust the liquid when the rice is done, to attain the right creamy consistency.*

4 to 5 cups chicken stock
½ ounce imported Italian or Polish dried
    mushrooms
4 tablespoons butter
½ cup minced onions
1½ cups Italian Arborio or long-grain Carolina
    rice
1 cup heavy cream
Salt and freshly ground white pepper to
    taste
½ cup freshly grated Parmesan cheese
2 to 3 tablespoons minced fresh parsley

In a heavy 3-quart saucepan, combine 2 cups of the chicken stock and the dried mushrooms. Bring to a boil, reduce heat, and simmer very slowly, covered, for 30 minutes. Line a sieve with a kitchen towel or layers of cheesecloth and drain the mushrooms and stock over a bowl; when cool, mince the mushrooms. Reserve the mushroom liquid.

In the same saucepan, melt the butter. Add the minced onions and cook them for 2 to 3 minutes, or until soft but not browned. Add the rice and stir for a minute or two to coat it well with the butter. Add 1 cup of stock, bring it to a boil, then reduce the heat and simmer the rice, stirring, until all stock has been ab-sorbed. Continue to add stock, 1 cup at a time, including the stock used to cook the mushrooms, cooking and stirring the rice until all the stock has been absorbed and the rice is tender but still slightly chewy.

Add the heavy cream and the reserved minced mushrooms and continue cooking until all the cream has been absorbed. Season with salt and pepper, add the Parmesan, garnish with parsley, and serve immediately. *Serves 4 to 6.*

Pasta with Golden Caviar

*C*aviar *makes a pretty plate and an elegant opening course for a special meal. The fresh tomato pasta contrasts nicely with the white sauce. If you are unable to find tomato pasta, make it by adding tomato paste to your favorite pasta recipe, or use spinach pasta for a variation.*

1½ cups heavy cream
1 pound fresh tomato pasta
1½ tablespoons chopped fresh chives (green
    onions can be substituted)
Freshly ground coarse black pepper
1 teaspoon fresh lemon juice
2 tablespoons (or more) golden caviar

Have all the ingredients ready. In a small, heavy saucepan, reduce the cream to 1 cup or until it coats a spoon. Cook the pasta in a large amount of boiling salted water for 1 to 3 minutes or until *al dente*. Drain; cover with the reduced cream. Toss in the chives, pepper, lemon juice, and mix well. Garnish with 1 teaspoon caviar per serving (at least!). *Serves 4 to 6.*

A welcome entry in the arena of ethnic foods, Picante is a taquería in the true Mexican style. Their fast food with soul is a far cry from the standard freeway taco. The food is similar to what you might purchase from a street vendor in Mexico, for example, marinated broiled meat in a soft corn tortilla with a freshly made salsa. The room is styled after a Western saloon, and the atmosphere is conducive to a family meal or an evening of drinking beer and listening to the weekend jazz band.

Compliments of

PICANTE TAQUERÍA & CANTINA

BERKELEY

Pollo Colorado

Chicken in Red Sauce

This dish is spicy, easy to prepare, and eminently satisfying.

One 3-pound chicken
4 to 5 large dried *ancho* or *pasilla* chilies
2 small red dried chilies
3 garlic cloves
1 tablespoon ground cumin
1 tablespoon dried oregano (optional)
Pinch ground cloves
3½ cups reserved chicken broth
3 tablespoons oil
2 tablespoons flour
Salt
Salsa Cruda, following

Place the chicken in a stockpot with cold water to cover. Boil gently, uncovered, for 1 hour; let the chicken cool in the broth. Reserve the broth and skim the fat. Skin, bone, and shred the chicken into small pieces.

Toast the dried chilies on a hot griddle or in a skillet to soften. Remove the seeds and stems, wearing gloves to prevent skin irritation. (If the dried chilies are not fairly fresh, they may be boiled at this point to soften them further.)

Place the chilies, garlic, cumin, oregano, and cloves in a blender or food processor with some of the chicken broth. Blend the mixture until puréed and add the remaining chicken broth to the purée.

Heat the oil in a large saucepan, add the flour, and cook until it bubbles. Add the chili-broth mixture slowly and cook until it thickens, stirring constantly. Add the shredded chicken meat, heat thoroughly, and serve with rice, beans, sour cream, corn tortillas, and Salsa Cruda, following. Warm the tortillas on a grill or by wrapping in foil in a hot oven. *Serves 4 to 6.*

Salsa Cruda

2 to 3 large tomatoes, chopped
½ onion, chopped
1 garlic clove, chopped (optional)
½ bunch cilantro, chopped
Salt to taste

Mix all the ingredients together well. Serve the sauce the day it is made. *Makes 1 to 1½ cups.*

Salsa Verde

Green Chili Sauce

Picante recommends serving this slightly tart and piquant sauce with red meat dishes, and, while we don't disagree, we found it was also good on broiled seafood.

8 fresh *tomatillos*
3 fresh Anaheim chilies
2 *serrano* chilies
1 small onion, chopped
Several sprigs of cilantro, chopped
Garlic (optional)
Salt (optional)
¼ cup water

Peel the papery husks from the tomatillos. In a hot skillet or on a grill, toast the husked tomatillos and chilies for about 10 minutes, or until softened, turning frequently. Remove any stems from the chilies. (Seed the chilies if a less spicy sauce is desired.)

Place the tomatillos, chilies, and all the remaining ingredients in a blender or food processor and purée. *Makes about 2 cups.*

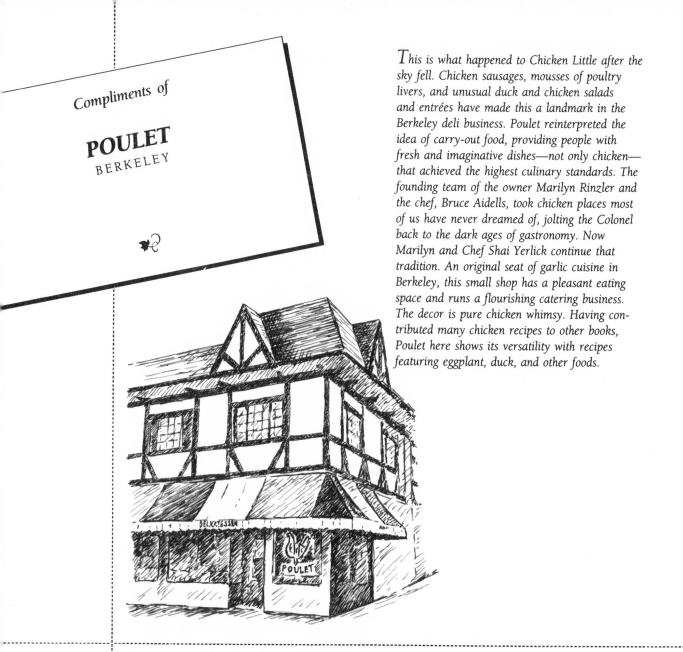

Compliments of

POULET

BERKELEY

This is what happened to Chicken Little after the sky fell. Chicken sausages, mousses of poultry livers, and unusual duck and chicken salads and entrées have made this a landmark in the Berkeley deli business. Poulet reinterpreted the idea of carry-out food, providing people with fresh and imaginative dishes—not only chicken—that achieved the highest culinary standards. The founding team of the owner Marilyn Rinzler and the chef, Bruce Aidells, took chicken places most of us have never dreamed of, jolting the Colonel back to the dark ages of gastronomy. Now Marilyn and Chef Shai Yerlick continue that tradition. An original seat of garlic cuisine in Berkeley, this small shop has a pleasant eating space and runs a flourishing catering business. The decor is pure chicken whimsy. Having contributed many chicken recipes to other books, Poulet here shows its versatility with recipes featuring eggplant, duck, and other foods.

Duck Liver Mousse

A simple recipe, and very good. The addition of apple is a nice touch.

½ apple, peeled and thinly sliced
1 large onion, coarsely chopped
2 cups (4 sticks) unsalted butter, at room temperature
2 pounds fresh duck livers
¼ cup dry sherry
¼ cup brandy
¼ cup heavy cream
Salt and pepper
Chopped fresh parsley or chopped toasted almonds

In a sauté pan or skillet, cook the apple and onion in 2 tablespoons of the butter until they are translucent and golden. Remove this mixture from the pan with a slotted spoon and place in a blender or food processor. Sauté the livers in the same pan for about 5 minutes, until it is browned outside but still pink inside (add more butter if necessary). Remove the livers with a slotted spoon and place in a blender or food processor with the apple-onion mixture. Deglaze the pan with the sherry.

Pour the pan drippings into the blender or food processor, add the brandy, cream, and remaining butter, and purée for 1 to 3 minutes, or until smooth. Add salt and pepper to taste. Pour into a mold and refrigerate for 5 hours. Unmold and garnish with chopped parsley or chopped toasted almonds. Serve with crackers or sliced baguettes. *Makes about 4 pounds.*

Spicy Eggplant

Good buffet or picnic fare, this dish improves over the course of a day or two. The chili content is adjustable. Don't overcook the eggplant, or it will fall apart by the time the dish is ready to serve. Chinese peppercorns, black bean sauce, and fermented black beans are all found in Chinese markets.

½ teaspoon Chinese peppercorns
2 tablespoons chopped fresh ginger
2 tablespoons minced garlic
½ teaspoon dried red pepper flakes
½ cup black bean sauce (if the bean sauce has red chilies, omit the pepper flakes)
2 tablespoons fermented black beans
¼ cup peanut oil
¼ cup soy sauce
2 tablespoons water
2 eggplants
Peanut oil
2 tablespons chopped cilantro
2 tablespoons chopped green onions

Roast the Chinese peppercorns in a 450° oven for 2 minutes or toast lightly in a sauté pan or skillet until they smoke a little. Grind them in a mortar. Purée the peppercorns, ginger, garlic, red pepper, bean sauce, and black beans in a blender or food processor. Add the ¼ cup peanut oil in a stream, then add the soy sauce and water.

Slice the eggplants ¾ inch thick lengthwise. Brush very lightly with oil, place on cookie sheets, and bake in a preheated 450° oven for 10 minutes, or until golden brown. Do not overcook. Cut the eggplant into 2-inch-square pieces and place in a serving dish in 1 layer. Spread the eggplant with the sauce and sprinkle with chopped cilantro and green onions; repeat the layering 4 or 5 times. Refrigerate and serve cold. *Serves 4 to 6.*

Seafood-Stuffed Summer Squash with Cilantro Sauce

This dish may seem a touch on the bizarre side, but it works beautifully. Use pattypan or cymling summer squash, or try a new variety called scaloppine squash.

12 pattypan or cymling squash
12 ounces angler fillet or other firm-fleshed
   white fish
¼ cup olive oil
Cilantro Sauce, following
¼ cup freshly grated Parmesan

Scoop out the inside of the squash to make room for the fish. Steam the hollowed-out squash for 3 minutes, then plunge them into cold water and drain. Sauté the fish in a sauté pan or skillet in very hot (smoking) olive oil until almost opaque in the center; remove from the pan and let cool. Fill each squash with a piece of the fish. Top with a little cilantro sauce and grated Parmesan cheese and brown under the broiler or in a very hot preheated oven (550°). Heat the remaining sauce and serve alongside the stuffed squash. *Serves 6 as an appetizer.*

Cilantro Sauce

2 bunches cilantro
1 bunch green onions
½ bunch parsley
¼ cup chopped garlic
⅓ cup fresh lemon juice
⅓ cup olive oil
½ cup heavy cream
Salt and pepper

Put the cilantro, onions, parsley, garlic, and lemon juice into a blender or food processor and blend into a paste. Add olive oil as necessary to keep things moving. Add the rest of the oil in a thin stream, then add the cream and season to taste with salt and pepper. *Makes about 1½ cups.*

Russ Riera, a local radio personality and restaurant critic, turned to Berkeley when he decided to open his own restaurant, responding to the absence of Northern Italian cuisine in this otherwise cuisine-rich city. He has transformed a cinder-block storefront with urban landscaping. Bright flower boxes adorn the front wall and the main dining room has a glass wall looking out onto an illuminated garden. The Northern Italian cooking of the chef, Lorenzo Pelayo, fills the menu with seafood soups and fresh pasta that, like all the bread, is made on the premises. Veal, prepared in a number of ways, is a specialty here.

Riera's is one of Berkeley's few small Italian restaurants, and it is a good choice when the urge for veal parmigiana or piccata hits.

Compliments of

RIERA'S
BERKELEY

Poached Fish with Piccata Sauce

This piccata sauce is a variant of beurre blanc, a member of the hot butter sauce family. (For more information on this group of sauces, see Basics.) The sauce and the poaching technique work well with other fish. Halibut, rockfish, tuna, and shark are particularly good with piccata sauce. Of course, the cooking time must be adjusted to the fish being used.

Poaching Liquid

3 carrots, cut into chunks
4 celery stalks, cut into chunks
2 large onions, chopped
4 cloves
12 peppercorns
1 to 2 bay leaves
½ bunch thyme (about 12 sprigs)
6 parsley sprigs
1½ to 2 quarts cold water
2 cups dry white wine
Juice of 2 lemons

Four 8-ounce whole trout or coho salmon

Piccata Sauce

6 tablespoons white wine vinegar
2 tablespoons minced shallots
1 cup reserved poaching liquid
6 tablespoons unsalted butter
2 tablespoons capers, drained
Salt and pepper

Combine the vegetables, spices, and herbs with the cold water in a large saucepan. Simmer for 20 minutes. Strain the liquid and place it in a 9-by-13-by-3-inch pan. Add the wine and lemon juice. Remove 1 cup of the poaching liquid and set it aside to make the sauce. Bring the remaining liquid to a boil, reduce heat, and add the fish. Let barely simmer for 10 minutes; with a spatula, carefully remove the fish to plates.

To make the sauce, place the vinegar and shallots in a small nonreactive saucepan. Add the reserved cup of poaching liquid. Boil down slowly, stirring to prevent any caramelizing along the insides of the pan, until only a tablespoonful or so of liquid remains. Over medium-low heat lightly whisk in the butter, half a tablespoon at a time, until a creamy, frothy sauce is formed. Add the capers and salt and pepper to taste, and pour over the fish. *Serves 4.*

NOTE: You can make the poaching liquid and the sauce ahead of time. Keep the sauce on a warm spot on the stove.

Wild Mushroom Lasagne

Good party or buffet fare, this rich lasagne is best prepared ahead of time and baked as needed.

2 ounces dried mushrooms (*porcini, cèpes, shiitakes*)
1½ cups hot water

Bechamel Sauce

3 cups milk
1 cup reserved mushroom-soaking liquid
4 tablespoons butter
½ cup flour
salt and pepper
Freshly grated nutmeg
Fresh lemon juice

1 pound fresh button mushrooms
1 pound fresh chanterelles (available fall and winter)
1 cup (2 sticks) butter, or 1 cup olive oil
Salt and pepper
Juice of 1 lemon
2 cups freshly grated Parmesan cheese
1½ cups feta cheese
1½ cups goat cheese
1 bunch thyme, chopped
1 bunch chives, chopped

2½ to 3 pounds fresh lasagne, or 1½ to 2 pounds dried lasagne

Soak the dried mushrooms in hot water to cover until they are soft. Remove the mushrooms and slice them, discarding any tough stems. Strain the soaking liquid and reserve for the bechamel sauce.

Prepare the bechamel sauce by combining the milk and mushroom-soaking liquid and bringing them to a simmer. Keep hot. In a heavy, nonreactive saucepan, melt the butter and add the flour. Let them foam together and cook for 2 to 3 minutes. Add the hot liquid all at once, beat well with a whisk, reduce the heat, and simmer the sauce for 20 to 30 minutes, until the raw taste of the flour is gone. Season the sauce with salt, pepper, nutmeg, and lemon juice to taste. Set the sauce aside, keeping it warm. In a large sauté pan or skillet, sauté all the mushrooms in the butter or olive oil until browned, including those you soaked earlier. Do this in small batches so that the mushrooms do not boil in their own liquid. Season them with salt and pepper and the juice of the lemon. Crumble the cheeses together. Mix the thyme and chives together.

Place the lasagne in a large amount of gently boiling salted water. Do not allow it to cook completely; it will finish in the oven. As you remove the pasta, chill it in cold water, then drain and toss with a little olive oil.

To assemble the lasagne, oil a 9-by-12-inch baking pan. Cover with a single layer of cooked pasta. Spread with a thin layer of bechamel sauce. Sprinkle with one-quarter of the Parmesan, followed by one-third of the mushrooms, one-third of the feta and goat cheeses, and one-third of the herbs. Repeat this process twice. Top with the last of the bechamel sauce and the remainder of the Parmesan. Bake in a preheated 400° oven for 30 minutes, or until golden brown and well heated. *Serves 8.*

Italian Wheat Bread

A very successful recipe that yields two loaves of flavorful, crusty, fine-grained bread. The key to the chewy crust of this bread is to bake the rounds on an open baking sheet; don't use bread pans.

½ cup lukewarm water (105° to 115°)
1 package (1 tablespoon) dry yeast
2 tablespoons honey
1 to 2 cups unbleached all-purpose flour
3 cups whole-wheat flour
1 cup semolina flour
2 teaspoons salt
2 cups hot water

Mix the lukewarm water with the yeast and honey. Sift the flours and the salt together, using only 1 cup of white flour. Add the water-yeast mixture to the flour, then mix in the hot water. Knead for 5 to 10 minutes by hand or 2 to 3 minutes with the dough hook of a mixer. If the mixture seems too soft, gradually add the remaining white flour. The final density should permit a well-formed ball of dough to just hold its shape or to very slowly spread a bit.

Place the dough in a large, lightly oiled bowl and cover with a damp cloth. Let the dough rise for 1 hour or so in a warm place until doubled in bulk. Knead again briefly and form the bread into 2 equal loaves. Place these loaves on a greased baking sheet. Let the loaves rise for another hour, or until doubled in bulk again. Bake in a preheated 400° oven for 15 minutes, then lower the heat to 350° for 25 minutes or until golden brown (this may take up to 40 minutes). The bread is ready when the loaves sound hollow when tapped on the bottom. *Makes 2 loaves.*

*S*mells of garlic, basil, and tomatoes envelop passersby on both sides of University Avenue, where the owners opened *Caffè Venezia*, then followed it a few years later with *Ristorante Venezia* across the street. In both restaurants, trompe l'oeil murals transport you to Venice. Diners may choose to rub elbows with other pasta eaters at the informal cafe, seated under lines of clothes hung from windows and balconies far above their heads, or they may eat the Italian version of nouvelle cuisine at the more formal ristorante. A unique feature of *Ristorante Venezia* is live opera recitals on Tuesday nights.

Compliments of

RISTORANTE VENEZIA
CAFFE VENEZIA
BERKELEY

Pasta alla Putanesca

Pasta with Piquant Tomato Sauce

This robust pasta is a great way to start a meal, or it can serve as a meal by itself. Freshly grated Parmigiano-Reggiano is excellent with this recipe. The heat of this dish can be adjusted to taste.

⅓ cup olive oil
9 anchovies
8 whole garlic cloves
¼ teaspoon dried red pepper flakes
4 medium ripe tomatoes, chopped and seeded
  (enough to make 3 cups of tomatoes), or
  one 28-ounce can tomatoes, chopped, with
  juice
12 Calamata olives, pitted and halved
2 teaspoons capers, drained
5 garlic cloves, chopped
⅓ cup chopped fresh parsley
1 tablespoon chopped fresh basil
½ to ¾ pound fresh pasta
Chopped fresh parsley

Heat the oil in a sauté pan or skillet. Add the anchovies and whole garlic cloves. Cook until the garlic cloves brown and the anchovies fall apart. Add the red pepper flakes and cook a few seconds more. Add the tomatoes, olives, and capers. Simmer the sauce for 30 minutes. Add the chopped garlic, parsley, and basil to the sauce and simmer a bit longer.

Cook the fresh pasta in plenty of boiling salted water for 2 to 3 minutes or until *al dente*. Toss with half of the sauce until well coated. Arrange the pasta on a platter and pour the remaining sauce on top. Sprinkle the chopped parsley over all. *Serves 4.*

Petti de Pollo Ripiene

Stuffed Chicken Breasts

Spinach, mushrooms and goat cheese marry well in this slightly difficult and filling dish. If your menu is extensive, reduce the recipe by half, serving only half a stuffed breast per guest. The full portion is very large.

½ cup unsalted butter
¼ pound mushrooms, sliced
½ pound spinach, chopped
1 cup ricotta cheese
1 egg
⅛ teaspoon ground nutmeg
6 ounces goat cheese
½ teaspoon salt
⅛ teaspoon ground black pepper
6 whole skinned and boned chicken breasts
  (leave them whole)
½ cup dry white wine
1 cup chicken stock
1 cup heavy cream

Melt 4 tablespoons of the butter in a sauté pan or skillet. Add the mushrooms and sauté until they are lightly browned and their moisture is absorbed. Add the spinach and sauté for 1 minute more. Remove the ingredients from the pan and drain in a sieve, pressing hard with the back of a large spoon to remove the excess moisture.

In a large bowl, mix the spinach and mushroom mixture, ricotta, egg, nutmeg, goat cheese, salt, and pepper.

Pound the chicken breasts between sheets of plastic wrap or waxed paper with the side of a cleaver until they are flattened but not broken. Place one-sixth of the mixture on each breast and spread it to 1 inch from the edges. Fold the chicken in half and close with toothpicks.

Melt the remaining 4 tablespoons of butter in a sauté pan or skillet. Add the chicken. Brown on one side, then turn. When the chicken is brown on the second side, add the wine and the stock, cover, and simmer for 7 to 10 minutes, until the chicken is just done (the flesh should spring back slightly when touched).

Remove the chicken and keep it hot. Add the cream to the liquid in the pan and reduce until thick enough to coat the back of a spoon. Adjust seasoning.

Remove the toothpicks and slice the chicken crosswise in about 4 slices each. Divide among 6 plates and strain a little of the sauce over each plate. *Serves 6.*

The Santa Fe Bar and Grill offers Western cuisine that features rotisserie-grilled meats, smoked fish, game, specialty items baked to order in the wood-burning oven, and homemade breads and pastas. The building was originally a train depot built by the Southern Pacific Railroad Company.

It was originally transformed into the Santa Fe Bar and Grill under the direction of some of Berkeley's best known chefs, most notably Mark Miller (now of the Coyote Café in Santa Fe, New Mexico) and Jeremiah Tower (now of Stars in San Francisco). The current owner and chef, Faz Poursohi, has recently remodeled the space which now combines the atmosphere of the early twenties with that of the American Southwest. With his experience in running successful restaurants in San Francisco, Faz has turned a languishing landmark into a thriving institution.

Fettuccine with Eggplant, Black Olives, and Feta Cheese

This simple pasta dish can be prepared in less than half an hour and could serve as a model on which to build variations.

4 Japanese eggplants
1 cup virgin olive oil
4 cloves garlic, chopped
1 cup Calamata olives
2 large tomatoes, roughly chopped
½ pound *fettuccine*
4 ounces feta cheese, grated
Salt and pepper

Cut the eggplant into 1-inch cubes or rounds and sauté in the oil with the garlic, olives, and tomatoes. At the same time cook the fettuccine. Drain the pasta well, mix with the sautéed vegetables, and add salt and pepper to taste. Divide onto plates and garnish with grated feta. *Serves 6.*

Grilled Pasilla Peppers with Salsa

Among the restaurant's favorite appetizers, what is essentially chiles rellenos *is given an unusual tang by the addition of the blue cheese. In the initial preparation, the chilies are more than merely blanched; they should be parboiled until they are soft enough to yield to pressure. Other-wise, when they are grilled, they will not be cooked before the cheese is melted, runny, and itself overcooked.*

4 to 8 *pasilla* peppers, depending upon size
4 ounces Roquefort cheese, grated
4 ounces white jack cheese, grated
4 ounces sharp Cheddar cheese, grated
Juice of 1 lemon

Salsa

Half a red onion
1 beefsteak tomato
1 avocado
Quarter bunch cilantro
1 *jalapeño* pepper
Juice of 2 lemons
¼ cup olive oil
Salt and pepper

To prepare the peppers, first cut a slice off the stalk end thick enough to form a cap. Reserve the caps and deseed the peppers. Parboil the peppers in boiling water for 4 to 5 minutes, chill in ice water, then dry them.

Mix the cheeses together with the lemon juice. Fill the peppers with the cheese mixture and recap. (A toothpick might help to hold it all together.)

Grill over mesquite for 3 to 5 minutes, until the cheese is melted. Serve with Salsa, following.

To make the Salsa, chop the onion, tomato, avocado, cilantro, and jalapeño pepper and mix well. Add the lemon juice and olive oil, and salt and pepper to taste. *Serves 4–6.*

Lime Tart

*T*his *refreshing dessert requires patience of the cook. The filling may convince you that it will never thicken. Persevere; it just takes time. The crust works beautifully and may be used for any dessert tart.*

Pie Shell

½ pound (2 sticks) butter
¼ cup sugar
½ teaspoon salt
2 cups flour
¼ cup cold water

Lime Filling

1 cup lime juice
1½ cups orange juice
8 eggs, beaten
10 ounces sugar (by weight)
4 ounces cream (by volume)

Make the pie shell first since it has to bake and cool before being filled. Mix the butter, sugar, salt, and flour together in a mixer with a paddle until crumbly. Add water just until the dough comes together. Do not overwork.

Press the dough into a 9- or 10-inch tart ring, cover with tinfoil, and weight with dry beans or aluminum pie weights.

Bake at 400° for 15 to 20 minutes, until the foil can be removed easily, then bake for another 15 minutes until the crust is golden brown.

To make the filling, mix the citrus juices, beaten eggs, sugar, and cream together and pass the mixture through a fine strainer. Cook in a double boiler until thick. This can take as long as 20 minutes, during which time you must stir constantly and keep the water in the lower part of the boiler from boiling too vigorously.

COMPLIMENTS OF THE CHEF

When Ellen Hyland and Jason Green decided to expand their sixteen-year-old catering company, the Sedona Grill was the fortunate result. The lunch and dinner menus change seasonally, but always feature a blend of traditional Southwestern ingredients with French and Californian cuisine. Southwestern rugs and plants accent the spacious dining area. (Fans of this restaurant will note that its original name, the Dakota Grill and Bar, has been recently changed.)

Compliments of

SEDONA GRILL & BAR
BERKELEY

Cold Roasted Eggplant with Ancho Chili Marinade, Sweet Peppers, and Cojita Cheese

*T*his *appetizer lends itself to dramatic presentation and is best served at room temperature. Use a light olive oil for the marinade. Toast the cumin seeds in a small dry pan over medium heat, keeping the seeds moving around. When they are quite brown, they should be transferred to a spice grinder of the coffee-mill type or, for a more authentic and sensual experience, use a mortar and pestle and enjoy the aromatic smoke from the hot crushed seeds. Cojita is a crumbly, salty cheese available from Mexican groceries. The leftover* ancho *chili marinade could be used for taco or enchilada sauce, added to chili, or frozen.*

2 medium eggplants
¾ cup olive oil plus extra for marinating and sautéeing
3 tablespoons dried oregano
½ pound dried *ancho* chilies
2 to 3 tablespoons lime juice
½ tablespoon garlic, finely chopped
2 teaspoons cumin seeds, toasted and ground
2 tablespoons cilantro, minced
Salt and pepper to taste
1 small red bell pepper, cut into very small dice
1 small yellow bell pepper, cut into very small dice
1 small *jalapeño* pepper, minced, with seeds
Half a sweet white or yellow onion, cut into very small dice

¼ cup aged *cojita* cheese (dried Mexican basket cheese), grated

Garnish

Lime wedges
Cilantro sprigs

Cut each eggplant into six wedges and marinate briefly (about 15 minutes) in ½ cup olive oil and the oregano. Roast in a 350° oven until the eggplant is cooked all the way through, about 45 minutes.

To make an ancho chili paste, toast the dried ancho chilies on a dry griddle or in a frying pan. They scorch easily; do not leave them unattended. When they are cool, remove the stems and seeds and soak for 30 minutes in warm water to cover. Drain and purée the softened chilies in a blender or food processor, adding enough soaking liquid to keep things moving. Pass the paste through a medium sieve to remove the skins. *Makes 1½ to 2 cups.*

Combine the ancho chili paste, ¾ cup olive oil, lime juice, garlic, toasted ground cumin, and cilantro. When the eggplant wedges have cooled, season them with salt and pepper and allow them to marinate in the chili paste and olive oil mixture for several hours or overnight.

Shortly before serving, sauté the red, yellow, and jalapeño peppers and the onion quickly in olive oil. Arrange wedges of eggplant on plates. Sprinkle with sautéed vegetables and grated cheese and garnish with lime wedges and cilantro. *Makes 8 generous first-course portions.*

Venison Picadillo

Traditionally, this New Mexican red chili stew is made with pork. Lamb could also be used. At Sedona it is served with crème fraîche *and Indian Fry Bread (recipe follows). The raisins or currants blend with the vinegar to give a sweet-sour character to the dish. Either can be adjusted to your taste.*

5 pounds venison leg meat, or shoulder, cut into ¾-inch dice
8 tablespoons garlic, minced
3 large white onions, cut into ½-inch dice
8 tablespoons vegetable oil
6 tablespoons cider vinegar
5 tablespoons honey
1 to 1½ cups *ancho* chili paste (see page 160)
3 cups golden raisins or zante currants
3 cups *piñon* nuts, toasted and blanched, or slivered almonds
1 tablespoon ground cinnamon
1 teaspoon ground cloves
3 tablespoons cumin seeds, toasted and ground
3 bay leaves
4 cups tomatoes, puréed
Chicken or venison stock to moisten
1 tablespoon ground *chili arbol*, or less if desired
Salt and pepper to taste

Mix the cubed venison with the garlic, onion, and oil and bake in a 350° oven for 1½ hours or more, until the venison has rendered its fat and has cooked all the way through.

Drain off the fat, return the venison to its pan, and add the cider vinegar, honey, chili paste, raisins or currants, nuts, cinnamon, cloves, cumin, bay leaves, and tomatoes. Moisten with some chicken or venison stock. Cook in a 350° oven for another 1½ hours, covered, taking care to stir the venison and moisten with more stock as needed.

Add the chili arbol during the last 15 minutes of cooking; it is quite piquant. Correct the seasoning, adding salt and pepper to taste. *Serves 8 generously.*

Indian Fry Bread

Similar to deep fried biscuits, this bread is decidedly not greasy; light and flavorful, it is a real asset to the Venison Picadillo.

2 cups unbleached white flour
2 teaspoons baking powder
1 teaspoon salt
1 tablespoon coriander seeds, toasted and
  ground
4 tablespoons scallion tops, chopped
⅔ to 1 cup milk
Peanut oil

Combine the dry ingredients and the scallion tops before adding the milk. Work the dough lightly and gather it into a mass.

Divide the dough into eight equal portions. Using a little flour to prevent sticking, form each portion into 3 balls. Flatten the balls into rounds.

Allow the dough to rest for 15 minutes before frying in hot peanut oil at 360° for roughly 2 minutes per side. Drain on paper towels. *Serves 8.*

Pine Nut and Apricot Tart

Crust

6 ounces butter, melted
2 scant cups all-purpose flour
¼ cup sugar
Pinch salt

Filling

½ pound dried apricots
¼ vanilla bean, split
½ cup sugar
¼ cup water
10 ounces cream cheese
3 egg yolks
½ cup pine nuts

Make the crust first. Combine all ingredients in a bowl. Butter a 9-inch tart pan. Press the dough evenly into the pan. Prebake the tart shell in a 425° oven for 15 to 20 minutes, until it is light golden brown.

While the tart shell is baking, make the filling. In a saucepan pour just enough water over the apricots and vanilla bean to cover. Bring to a boil and simmer over low heat until the apricots are soft. Drain off excess water. Remove the vanilla bean. Purée the apricots in a food processor or chop fine by hand. Spread on the bottom of the prebaked tart shell.

Boil the sugar and water together for 2 minutes.

In a food processor with a metal blade attachment process the cream cheese and the egg yolks until smooth. Add the sugar water and process again. Pour the filling over the apricots and sprinkle the pine nuts over the top. Bake in a 350° oven for 30 to 40 minutes or until the center is set and golden brown. Chill for at least an hour before cutting. *Serves 12.*

This is where many Berkeley chefs come to eat after work. The next day, you may find their menus reflecting what they have eaten here. This well-respected restaurant occupies a former bar called "Harry's Pearl of the Orient." The vinyl booths, gas fireplace, and dance floor remain, but the past ends there. Stunning Thai dishes balancing hot, sour, and salty flavors with accents of the exotic (lemon grass, galangal, coconut milk) send diners diving for their Thai beers, mopping their brows, and ordering seconds. Almost unassisted, this restaurant sparked a local cult of chili lovers. Not all the dishes are incendiary, however, and some feature fascinating complexities of flavor without chilies.

Compliments of

SIAM CUISINE
BERKELEY

Tom Kar Gai

Thai Chicken Soup

This sublimely simple chicken soup, rich with coconut milk and piquant with lime, would be an exotic beginning for any meal, or it could be the star of a simple meal. Much of its charm comes from cooking the chicken accurately. It should be just done. Do not cook the soup beyond the point at which it comes to a boil. Those who like chili will enjoy a sprinkling of red pepper flakes.

1½ cups unsweetened coconut milk
2 cups chicken broth
2 tablespoons fresh *galangal*, chopped, then puréed in a blender
4 ounces boneless chicken breast, cut in finger-sized pieces
¼ cup sliced bamboo shoots, drained
3 tablespoons fish sauce
3 tablespoons fresh lime juice
Cilantro sprigs or dried red pepper flakes

In a large saucepan, heat the coconut milk with the broth and the galangal. Do not boil. Add the chicken, bamboo shoots, fish sauce, and lime juice. Heat the mixture slowly until it just comes to a boil. Serve with a garnish of cilantro sprigs or red pepper flakes. *Serves 4.*

Salty Beef

Garnished with a sprinkle of red pepper flakes and wedges of lime, this dish is a knockout! There is an unusual technique involved here, a marinating process wherein the marinade is dried out of the beef, a trick the recipe tester enjoyed learning.

To fit this dish into an Asian menu is no problem, but a Western menu may require some insulation in the form of an intervening course of cold fish or perhaps an ice. It would also be interesting to serve some fresh tropical fruit with the beef.

Don't be put off by the "exotic" smell of the meat as it marinates in the fish sauce. The aroma dissipates upon frying. (See the Ingredients section on fish sauce.)

1 pound flank steak
1 tablespoon sugar
6 tablespoons fish sauce
2 tablespoons ground coriander
2 cups vegetable oil
Dried red pepper flakes (optional)
Lime wedges
Cilantro sprigs

Thinly slice the flank steak at an angle across the grain. Place the slices in one layer in an ovenproof pan. Mix together the sugar, fish sauce, and coriander and pour over the flank steak. Place in a preheated 175° to 200° oven and leave until the meat is dry, turning occasionally; this will take 3 to 4 hours.

When ready to serve, heat the oil in a deep, heavy pot. Fry the flank steak in the oil, turning until the meat is browned. Remove the beef, drain on paper towels to remove excess oil, and serve immediately, garnished, if desired, with red pepper flakes, lime wedges, and cilantro. *Serves 4 as an appetizer.*

Chicken Curry

Very hot, very complex, very unusual—these are the only ways to describe this delicious curry. You'll just have to try it. The hardest part is finding the ingredients—they are available in Asian markets.

6 to 7 small dried red peppers
1 teaspoon salt
1 tablespoon sliced fresh or dried lemon grass
1 teaspoon dried *galangal* (*laos* powder)
1 teaspoon dried lime peel
1 tablespoon ground coriander
3½ tablespoons chopped garlic
½ small red onion, sliced
1 teaspoon ground fennel
5½ cups unsweetened coconut milk
2 cups water
3 to 4 chicken breast halves, skinned, boned, and cut into 1-inch dice
2 tablespoons fish sauce
1 cup sliced bamboo shoots
¼ cup basil leaves
3 chopped *jalapeño* chilies
¼ cup crumbled dried lime leaves

Place the dried peppers in boiling water to cover for 1 minute, then seed and chop them. Mix with the salt, lemon grass, galangal, lime peel, coriander, garlic, red onion, and fennel. Set aside.

In a large saucepan, boil the coconut milk with the 2 cups water over low heat for 5 to 10 minutes. Set aside ½ cup. In a wok or skillet, stir-fry the chili mixture with the ½ cup coconut milk until well mixed. Add the chicken and the remaining coconut milk. Stir-fry until boiling, then add the fish sauce and bamboo shoots. Transfer to a platter and sprinkle with basil leaves, chopped chilies, and lime leaves. *Serves 3 to 4.*

Chicken with Sweet Basil

This dish is incendiary; the wine has not been created that could stand up to it. Strictly a beer-drinking proposition! Some hot-food advice: Cook plenty of rice. It quenches the fire better than beer or water. Also be warned that sautéing chili peppers, as in this recipe, produces very pungent fumes.

¼ cup vegetable oil
½ to 1 teaspoon dried red pepper flakes or to taste
2 teaspoons chopped garlic
1 pound boneless chicken, cut into ½-inch by 2-inch strips
4 to 6 *jalapeño* peppers, cut lengthwise and seeded
3 tablespoons fish sauce
Leaves from 4 stems of basil

Heat the oil in a sauté pan or skillet. Add the red pepper and garlic and stir quickly so they will not burn; add the chicken immediately. Add the jalapeños and sauté until the chicken is half done, about 2 to 3 minutes (the chicken should be lightly brown, but still soft). Add the fish sauce and cook 2 more minutes. Add the basil leaves, stir twice, remove from the heat, and serve. *Serves 4.*

*Y*ou can't discuss Berkeley restaurants without including Spenger's. Big, noisy, and boisterous, Spenger's retains that after-the-Big-Game atmosphere year round. It is enormously popular, and dinner parties are often made up in order to take advantage of the reservation policy, which requires a minimum of six diners. Otherwise, waits up to an hour are not uncommon, and Spenger's has a huge bar area to accommodate waiting patrons until a table is available. Once you are seated, service is efficient, portions are ample and reasonably priced, and the supply of sourdough bread is endless. No desserts are offered at Spenger's, but no one has ever left hungry!

Cold Poached Salmon with Cucumber–Sour Cream Sauce

A simple, basic recipe for a standby of buffet entertaining. Its quality depends on the quality of the salmon used.

6 salmon fillets, 5 to 8 ounces each, or one
   3-pound section or whole fish
Juice of 1 lemon
4 to 6 bay leaves
Pinch of salt

Cucumber–Sour Cream Sauce

1 large cucumber, peeled, seeded, and
   chopped
2 cups sour cream, at room temperature
½ onion, chopped
Pinch of salt

Place the salmon in a large deep pan and cover with cold water. Add the lemon juice, bay leaves, and salt. Bring to a boil, lower heat, and poach for about 10 minutes depending on the thickness of the fish—a small whole salmon should cook for about 20 minutes. The fish should be a bit translucent in the center when done. Carefully remove the fish with a slotted spatula and let it cool.

Mix together all the ingredients for the sauce and serve it with the salmon. *Serves 6.*

The menus at Thornhill Café, opened in 1986 by Chai and Diane Butsangde, reflect Chai's French training and his Thai heritage. The dishes are prepared in a French style infused with Thai herbs and seasonings. Although the dining room is small, large tiled windows and mirrors bring the Montclair hills into view and convey a sense of spaciousness.

Hawaiian Ono Sautéed with Butter, Lime, and Toasted Shallots

This dish is bound to be a hit. The savory shallots blend beautifully with the sharpness of lime juice. Ono is a firm, moist fish, reminiscent of a very moist seabass. Almost any firm flavorful fish would benefit from this treatment, particularly halibut, seabass, or swordfish.

Toasted Shallots

2 shallots, coarsely chopped
1 tablespoon butter
4 ono fillets, 6 to 8 ounces each
2 tablespoons vegetable oil
Juice of 2 limes
1 teaspoon *nam pla* (Thai fish sauce)

Sauté the shallots over a gentle fire until very brown, but do not burn. Drain on a paper towel. Do not hesitate to make extra; it keeps well refrigerated.

Sear the ono fillets in hot oil for a minute or two. Turn the fish, reduce the heat to medium, add the lime juice, fish sauce, and toasted shallots. Cook for another minute or so, until the fish is done to taste. Remove the fish and reduce the sauce, if necessary. *Serves 4.*

Four-Flavors Fish

Derived from a recipe for a crisply fried, small, whole fish, this dish uses fillets. Spicy, tart, sweet, and savory, the dish is a charmer.

4 rockfish fillets, 6 to 8 ounces each
2 shallots, sliced
1 or 2 *serrano* chilies, seeded and julienned
2 teaspoons palm sugar (available in Thai groceries, or substitute brown sugar)
Half a red onion, thinly sliced
Half a medium red bell pepper, julienned
Half a medium green pepper, julienned
½ teaspoon *nam pla* (Thai fish sauce)
Lime juice

Brown the fillets in very hot oil, add the shallots and chilis and brown slightly. Add the palm sugar, mix, and then add the vegetables. Sauté until the vegetables are tender but still crisp and the fish is cooked. Remove the fish. Season to taste with fish sauce and lime juice. *Serves 4.*

TOURELLE CAFÉ AND RESTAURANT

LAFAYETTE

*T*ourelle occupies an old vine-covered building with a tower (for which the restaurant is named). The dining area looks onto a lovely courtyard with a fountain. Opened in 1985 by Annette Esser (former owner of A La Carte), Tourelle brings diversity to the East Bay's Contra Costa County with its double menu; the provincial-style café serves mesquite-grilled foods and pizza from a wood-fired hearth and a formal French dining room offers à la carte lunches and fixed-price, five-course dinners.

Salmon Fillet in a Leek Collar with Salmon Soufflé

In an elegant if somewhat elaborate presentation, the salmon fillet is wrapped with blanched leek, topped with a rich salmon mousse, gently baked, and sauced with a beurre blanc. *The final, very classically French result resembles* sushi *in appearance.*

1 large leek
2 eight-ounce salmon fillets (each measuring approximately 6 by 3 inches and 1 inch thick)
1 tablespoon brandy
2 egg whites
1 tablespoon lemon juice
⅛ teaspoon allspice
Salt and pepper
1 cup heavy cream
1 tablespoon butter

Beurre Blanc

4 shallots, finely chopped (enough for ¼ cup)
½ cup white wine
¼ cup white wine vinegar
½ pound butter, cut into small pieces

Garnish

Salmon or golden caviar

Wash and blanch a 12-inch strip of leek, green part only, and set aside.

Cut a third off each of the steaks lengthwise, then cut these strips in cubes and purée in a food processor. Add the brandy, egg whites, lemon juice, allspice, and salt and pepper to taste. The mixture should be very smooth and slightly underseasoned. (The flavors will be more pronounced when the mixture is cooked and warm.) Transfer to a mixing bowl and gradually mix in the cream with a rubber spatula. Do not allow the mixture to warm up; work over ice if possible, and do not overmix or the mousse will be grainy.

To assemble (this may be done 8 hours in advance), place the fillets on their sides and roll them up like a pinwheel.

Melt the butter, paint the blanched and dried strips of leek with it, and stick them to the sides of the pinwheels, building up a 2-inch collar. Next, cut a piece of waxed paper, butter it, and wrap it around the leek collar to secure it. The paper should come an inch above the leek. Fill the cavity with the mousse, cover with a square of buttered waxed paper, and chill.

To make the *beurre blanc*, put the shallots, white wine, and vinegar into a nonreactive saucepan and reduce to a syrup. Over low heat, gradually whisk in the butter and keep warm, but not hot. (See Basics for details of the technique of making a *beurre blanc*.)

Place the assembled salmon in a buttered, ovenproof pan with a little white wine. Bake in a preheated 350° oven for 15 to 20 minutes, until the mousse tests firm with a small knife or skewer. Remove the waxed paper, place on a plate, sauce with *beurre blanc*, and garnish with salmon or golden caviar. *Serves 2.*

Roquefort and Apple Flan

This is a rich and unconventional dessert, an appropriate finale to a daring menu. And there is no reason not to substitute pears and Gorgonzola for apple and Roquefort. The flavors improve when the flan is made a day in advance.

Caramel

½ cup pear vinegar (or substitute apple cider vinegar)
½ cup orange juice
½ cup sugar

Apples and Custard

2 tart green apples
2 tablespoons butter
10 ounces cream
2 eggs
Pinch of nutmeg
Pinch of salt and pepper
4 ounces Roquefort cheese, grated

Garnish

Toasted walnuts or pecans
Fresh apple

To make the caramel, combine the vinegar, orange juice, and sugar in a small, heavy saucepan and cook over medium-high heat until thickened and brown. While the caramel is still warm enough to flow, but not smoking hot, coat 6 eight-ounce soufflé or custard molds with 1½ tablespoons of the caramel mixture. If the caramel is too thick, add a little water, warm the mixture, and stir until smooth.

Peel and slice the apples and sauté them in the butter. Line the molds with the sautéed slices and top with half of the Roquefort.

Thoroughly mix the cream, eggs, nutmeg, and salt and pepper. Cook over simmering water in a double boiler until just slightly thickened and immediately add the remaining cheese. Be careful not to overcook.

Fill the molds and bake, at 325°, in a water bath, covered with buttered parchment or waxed paper, for 35 to 45 minutes, until set. Pierce the flan with a paring knife to test.

Serve with toasted walnuts or pecans and slices of fresh apple. *Serves 6.*

*A*ndronico's Park and Shop opened its first market in Berkeley in 1929. Vasilio's Kitchen was opened in 1984 as a part of Park and Shop's ambitious renovation of all its stores. Vasilio's brings to Berkeley a deli catering to California tastes. Under the direction of Daniel Strongin, the kitchen turns out an enormous selection of salads and hot dishes, many of which change daily.

Compliments of

VASILIO'S KITCHEN
BERKELEY

Hunan-Style Smoked Chicken and Pasta Salad

This wonderful salad is at its best when eaten as soon as it is dressed.

Dressing

1½ tablespoons sugar
1 tablespoon chopped garlic
1 tablespoon chopped ginger
1⅓ cups peanut oil
⅓ cup sesame oil
¼ cup hot chili oil
½ cup regular or light soy sauce
¾ cup black soy sauce
½ cup black vinegar

Salad

1 pound cooked *fusilli* or *rotelle* noodles
1 cup cubed smoked chicken (roasted chicken
   may be substituted)
1 cup sliced carrots
1 bunch scallions, sliced diagonally
½ cup red cabbage, shredded
1 cup cooked asparagus, sliced (snow peas
   may be substituted)
2 *serrano* chili peppers, chopped

To make the dressing, combine the sugar, garlic, and ginger. Add the peanut, sesame, and hot chili oils and whisk in the soy sauces and vinegar. Allow to stand for 15 minutes before using. *Makes about 3⅔ cups.*

To assemble, toss all the salad ingredients together, then dress with enough dressing to coat well. You may have extra dressing. *Serves 6.*

Spicy Turkey Salad

This is a very zesty salad. You can temper the degree of hotness by using a light hand with the pepper flakes or chili oil.

1 pound turkey breast, cooked and cubed
¼ bunch fresh cilantro, chopped
½ cup chopped tomatoes
¼ cup diced red onion
1 *serrano* chili pepper, chopped (optional)
Cilantro sprigs for garnish

Dressing

1 teaspoon red pepper flakes
1 teaspoon sesame oil
1 teaspoon hot chili oil
1 tablespoon rice wine vinegar
½ cup homemade mayonnaise

Combine all the ingredients. Chill and serve garnished with cilantro. *Serves 4.*

Thai Cucumber Salad

Quintessential California deli fare, this salad is easily assembled and sparkles with fresh flavors and unusual ingredients.

3 Japanese cucumbers
1 stalk celery
1 yellow squash
Half a carrot
Quarter red onion
1 or 2 *serrano* chilies
Fresh ginger
1 clove garlic
½ teaspoon lemon grass
Zest of half a lemon
Half a bunch fresh basil leaves, trimmed of
    stems
2 tablespoons peanut oil
1½ teaspoons rice wine vinegar
Nam pla (Thai fish sauce)

Trim the ends from the cucumber, split lengthwise, and slice on the diagonal. Julienne all the vegetables. Slice the chilies into paper-thin rounds. (Don't forget to wash your hands NOW!) Chop equal amounts of ginger and garlic together, mince the lemon grass and lemon zest, and cut the basil into a chiffonnade by rolling the leaves up together and shredding them thinly. Toss the salad ingredients and dress with peanut oil, vinegar, and fish sauce. *Serves 4 to 6.*

Compliments of

WALKER'S PIE SHOP
ALBANY

*W*alker's is a timeless touch of Americana. This neighborhood institution serves unassuming, moderately priced meals to its loyal customers. Take-out cream pies and berry pies are a mainstay. Dinner at eight may be the fashion elsewhere in town, but that is the hour when this home-style restaurant begins to lock up for the night. Tastes and politics are debated endlessly in Berkeley, but no one there would challenge the staying power of Walker's.

Rhubarb Pie

Rhubarb's acidity and astringency make it a good choice to end a heavy menu, and rhubarb pie is a natural for vanilla ice cream.

1 recipe Pie Dough, page 83
1 cup sugar
¼ teaspoon ground nutmeg
½ teaspoon salt
1 tablespoon cornstarch
1 tablespoon tapioca
¼ cup water, if using fresh rhubarb
4 cups rhubarb, fresh or thawed frozen
1 tablespoon butter

Prepare the pie dough. Use 1 circle of dough to line a 10-inch pie pan. Roll the second dough ball to use as the top crust. Mix the sugar, nutmeg, salt, cornstarch, and tapioca together in a bowl, adding the ¼ cup water if using fresh rhubarb. Stir this mixture into the rhubarb. Pour the rhubarb into the pie shell. Dot with butter and cover with the top crust, crimping the edges of the two crusts together. Slash the top or cut a center hole to vent the steam while cooking. Bake for 45 to 55 minutes in a preheated 375° oven, until the top crust is golden brown. *Makes 6 to 8 servings.*

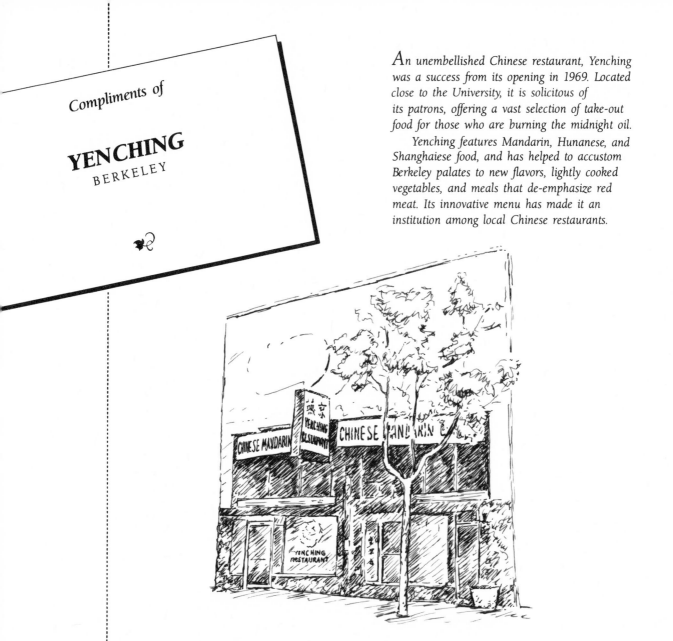

Compliments of

YENCHING
BERKELEY

*A*n unembellished Chinese restaurant, Yenching was a success from its opening in 1969. Located close to the University, it is solicitous of its patrons, offering a vast selection of take-out food for those who are burning the midnight oil.

Yenching features Mandarin, Hunanese, and Shanghaiese food, and has helped to accustom Berkeley palates to new flavors, lightly cooked vegetables, and meals that de-emphasize red meat. Its innovative menu has made it an institution among local Chinese restaurants.

Minced "Squab" Appetizer

An imitation of squab that is actually reminiscent of the real thing, and great fun to eat. The hardest part of the recipe is cutting everything to the right size.

4 ounces dried black mushrooms
½ cup canned water chestnuts, drained
½ cup sliced bamboo shoots, drained
8 ounces boneless chicken breast
5¼ cups vegetable oil
2 teaspoons soy sauce
2 teaspoons rice wine or dry sherry
1 teaspoon Oriental sesame oil
½ teaspoon chopped garlic
½ teaspoon chopped fresh ginger
1 green onion, chopped
1-ounce package bean threads
12 red leaf lettuce leaves

Soak the mushrooms in warm water to cover until softened, about 30 minutes. Drain; save the liquid for another use. Mince the mushrooms, water chestnuts, and bamboo shoots. Chop the chicken breast into pieces the size of rice kernels. Preheat a medium-sized wok with ¼ cup of the vegetable oil.

In a medium-sized bowl, mix the minced mushrooms, water chestnuts, bamboo shoots, and chicken with the soy sauce, rice wine, and sesame oil.

Sauté the garlic, ginger, and green onion in the wok for 1 minute. Add the chicken mixture to the wok. Sauté, stirring vigorously, until there is no pinkness in the chicken.

In a deep, heavy pot, heat the remaining 5 cups of vegetable oil until almost smoking. Deep-fry the bean threads; they will puff up and double in size immediately. Remove from the pot with a slotted spoon and drain them on paper towels.

Place the fried bean threads on a platter and spoon the chicken mixture on top. Place the red leaf lettuce leaves on a second platter. To serve, place 1 tablespoon cooked chicken mixture and bean threads onto 1 lettuce leaf, roll up, and eat pancake style. *Serves 2.*

Mandarin Green Beans, Szechwan-Style

*A*side *from the trouble of deep-frying, this is an easy dish to execute—and easier to eat! It might be worthwhile to try steaming the beans rather than frying them. The bean paste sauce is available in Chinese markets.*

2 pounds Blue Lake green beans or Chinese long beans
5 cups vegetable oil
1 small piece fresh ginger, chopped
2 green onions, chopped
1 tablespoon hot bean-paste sauce
1 tablespoon sugar
½ tablespoon salt
1 tablespoon dry sherry
2 tablespoons soy sauce
1 tablespoon Oriental sesame oil
½ cup water

Cut the green beans on the diagonal into 3- to 4-inch lengths. In a deep, heavy pot, heat the vegetable oil until almost smoking. Deep-fry the beans in the hot oil for 4 minutes, remove with a slotted spoon, and drain on paper towels.

In a small bowl mix the ginger, green onions, hot bean paste, sugar, salt, sherry, soy sauce, and sesame oil together. Place the beans, water, and bean paste mixture into a sauté pan or skillet. Cook and stir for 3 minutes over high heat and serve. *Serves 6 to 8.*

*T*raveling *together in Europe for two years as fashion models, Zachary Zachowski and Barbara Gabel pursued an unlikely diversion in their spare time: perfecting the recipe for Chicago-style stuffed pizza. When they finally returned to the United States, they decided their product was ready for the public market, and they opened a restaurant to showcase it. Even native Chicagoans praise the menu here. The success of the first pizzeria has led to a second one at the other end of town, just across the Berkeley city limits. Further proof that eclectic influences can be extended to all cuisines: Zachary's stuffed spinach pizza with pesto sauce.*

Compliments of

ZACHARY'S
CHICAGO PIZZA

BERKELEY

OAKLAND

Stuffed Pizza

Here is a unique pizza, a sort of Chicago-style calzone. The tricky part is making sure the top crust, which cooks under a layer of tomato sauce, is cooked through. We determined in testing that rolling the top crust thinner than the bottom is helpful. We also recommend filling the pizza with something more than just cheese, as it helps to fill the pan and gives the crust some support, not to mention making a more interesting pizza.

Crust

1 tablespoon sugar
1 package (1 tablespoon) active dry yeast
2 cups lukewarm water (105° to 115°)
¼ cup vegetable oil
4 to 6 cups unbleached all-purpose flour

Tomato Sauce

2 tablespoons olive oil
1 garlic clove, minced
One 28-ounce can crushed tomatoes and added purée
1½ teaspoons minced fresh oregano
1½ teaspoons minced fresh basil
¼ teaspoon freshly ground black pepper

2½ cups shredded whole-milk mozzarella cheese
¼ cup freshly grated Parmesan cheese
¼ cup freshly greated Romano cheese
Spinach Pesto Sauce, following (optional)

To make the crust, dissolve the sugar and yeast in the water in a large bowl; let stand until bubbly. Stir in the oil. Stir in 4 cups of the flour until smooth. Stir in the remaining flour as needed to form a stiff dough. Knead on a lightly floured surface until smooth and elastic. Put into a greased bowl. Turn the dough once to coat the top with oil and allow to rise until doubled in size.

To make the tomato sauce, heat the olive oil in a large saucepan and sauté the garlic lightly. Stir in the tomatoes, oregano, basil, salt, and pepper. Simmer for 30 minutes or until very thick.

Punch down the dough and let it rest for 10 minutes. On a lightly floured surface, roll two-thirds of the dough into a 16-inch circle. Fit this into a 12- to 14-inch deep-dish pizza pan. Make sure that the dough is pressed against the sides of the pan and that it extends over the rim.

Mix the cheeses and spread evenly over the dough. Roll the remaining dough on a lightly floured surface to form a 14-inch circle. Place over the filled dough. Seal the edges of the dough together and cut off any excess dough near the top rim of the pan.

Pour the tomato sauce over the top layer of dough and, if desired, top with spinach pesto sauce. Bake in a preheated 450° oven for 25 to 30 minutes, or until the crust is golden. *Serves 6.*

Spinach Pesto Sauce

¼ cup pine nuts
2 to 3 garlic cloves, chopped
¾ cup olive oil
1 cup chopped spinach
¾ cups basil leaves
¼ cup freshly grated Parmesan cheese
¼ cup freshly grated Romano cheese
Salt and pepper

Grind the pine nuts, garlic, and olive oil in a blender or food procesor until smooth. Add the spinach and basil and purée until smooth. Then add the cheeses, finishing the mixing by hand if the pesto is too thick for the machine to handle. Add salt and pepper to taste. *Makes about 2 cups, enough for 2 large pizzas.*

NOTE: This sauce may be frozen, but it is best to freeze without the cheeses added.

Lois Marcus, Paul T. Johnston, and Ruth Dorman

RESTAURANT INDEX

A LA CARTE
1453 Dwight Way
Berkeley
548-2322

AUGUSTA'S
2955 Telegraph Avenue
Berkeley
548-3140

BAY WOLF RESTAURANT
3853 Piedmont
Oakland
655-6004

BETTE'S OCEANVIEW DINER
1807A Fourth Street
Berkeley
644-3230

BETTE'S-TO-GO
1807 Fourth Street
Berkeley
548-9494

BOMBAY CUISINE
2006 Ninth Street
Berkeley
843-9601

BREAD GARDEN
2912 Domingo Avenue
Berkeley
548-3122

BRITT-MARIE'S
1369 Solano Avenue
Albany
527-1314

BROADWAY TERRACE CAFÉ
5891 Broadway Terrace
Oakland
652-4442

CAFÉ FANNY
1601 San Pablo Avenue
Berkeley
524-5447

CAFÉ GLENDA
1897 Solano Avenue
Berkeley
527-7499

CAFÉ PASTORAL
2160 University Avenue
Berkeley
540-7514

CHEESE BOARD
1504 Shattuck Avenue
Berkeley
549-3183

CHEZ PANISSE
1517 Shattuck Avenue
Berkeley
548-5525

CHRISTOPHER'S CAFÉ
1843 Solano Avenue
Berkeley
526-9444

CLAREMONT HOTEL
Pavillion Room
41 Tunnel Road
Berkeley
843-3000

COCOLAT
1481 Shattuck Avenue
Berkeley
843-3265

FATAPPLE'S
1346 Martin Luther King Jr. Way
Berkeley
526-2260

FOURTH STREET GRILL
1820 Fourth Street
Berkeley
849-0526

GERTIE'S CHESAPEAKE BAY CAFÉ
1919 Addison Street
Berkeley
841-2722

GIOVANNI'S
2420 Shattuck Avenue
Berkeley
843-6678

GULF COAST OYSTER BAR AND RESTAURANT
736 Washington
Oakland
839-6950

HUNAN PALACE
1556 Solano Avenue
Albany
525-2330

INN KENSINGTON
293 Arlington Avenue
Kensington
527-5919

KATHLEEN'S DOYLE STREET CAFÉ
5515 Doyle Street
Emeryville
547-3552

LA CRÈME DE LA CRÈME
5362 College Avenue
Oakland
420-8822

LALIME'S
1329 Gilman Street
Berkeley
527-9838

LIPPZ BISTRO
2211 Clayton Road
Concord
821-1363

METROPOLE
2271 Shattuck Avenue
Berkeley
848-3080

MUDD'S
10 Boardwalk
San Ramon
837-9387

NADINE RESTAURANT
2400 San Pablo Avenue
Berkeley
549-2807

NAKAPAN
1921 Martin Luther King Jr. Way
Berkeley
548-3050

NAN YANG
301 8th Street
Oakland
465-6924

NORMAN'S
College and Alcatraz Avenues
Berkeley
655-5291

**OLIVETO CAFÉ AND
RESTAURANT**
5655 College Avenue
Oakland
547-5356

OMNIVORE
3015 Shattuck Avenue
Berkeley
848-4346

PANINI
2115 Allston Way
Berkeley
849-0405

PASTA SHOP
5655 College Avenue
Oakland
547-4005

PICANTE TAQUERÍA & CANTINA
1328 Sixth Street
Berkeley
526-9779

POULET
1685 Shattuck Avenue
Berkeley
845-5932

RIERA'S
1539 Solano Avenue
Berkeley
527-1467.

RISTORANTE VENEZIA
1902 University Avenue
Berkeley
644-3093

CAFFÈ VENEZIA
1903 University Avenue
Berkeley
849-4681

SANTA FE BAR AND GRILL
1310 University Avenue
Berkeley
841-4740

SEDONA GRILL AND BAR
2086 Allston Way
Berkeley
841-3848

SIAM CUISINE
1181 University Avenue
Berkeley
548-3278

SPENGER'S FISH GROTTO
1919 Fourth Street
Berkeley
845-7771

THORNHILL CAFÉ
5761 Thornhill Drive
Oakland
339-0646

**TOURELLE CAFÉ AND
RESTAURANT**
3565 Mount Diablo Boulevard
Lafayette
284-3565

VASILIO'S KITCHEN
1850 Solano Avenue
Berkeley
524-0513

WALKER'S PIE SHOP
1491 Solano Avenue
Albany
525-4647

YENCHING
2017 Shattuck Avenue
Berkeley
848-2200

ZACHARY'S CHICAGO PIZZA
5801 College Avenue
Oakland
655-6385

RECIPE INDEX

APPETIZERS/FIRST COURSES

Axonometric Appetizer   62
Bon Bon Chicken   96
Chicken Liver Mousse Pâté   88
Cold Roasted Eggplant with Ancho Chili Marinade, Sweet Peppers, and Cojita Cheese   160
Duck Liver Mousse   147
Eggplant "Cake" with Tomato "Jelly"   103
Fresh Corn Timbale with Red Pepper Vinaigrette   49
Leek Terrine with Achiote Vinaigrette Appetizer   93
Minced "Squab" Appetizer   179
Mock Boursin (Herbed Cream Cheese)   64
Mushroom and Pecan Pâté   133
Onion Uthapa (Onion Pancake)   40
Roasted Garlic and Almond Spread   90
Roasted Peppers with Creamed Feta   45
Salty Beef   164
Seafood-Stuffed Summer Squash with Cilantro Sauce   148
Topinka   45

BEEF/LAMB/VEAL/VENISON

Boeuf Gribiche (Beef with Gribiche Sauce)   113
Braised Lamb Shanks with Fresh Shellbeans, Tomato, and Herbs   130
Burmese Curried Beef Stew   124
Dry-Aged New York Steak with Roquefort Cheese Sauce   61
Green Curry Beef   122
Marinated Grilled Leg of Lamb   106
Rack of Lamb Assyrian   vii
Sautéed Marinated Lamb with Thai Peppers, Red Onion, and Hoisin Sauce   74
Venison Picadillo   161

BREADS

Asiago Bread   64
Cinnamon-Swirl Loaves   42

Czech Bread   46
Fresh Fruit Bran Muffins   100
German Potato Bread   42
Indian Fry Bread   162
Italian Wheat Bread   152
Sticky Buns   43

CHICKEN AND DUCK
Barbecued Chicken with Cabbage Salad   121
Chicken Curry   165
Chicken with Sweet Basil   165
Duck Sausage Wrapped in Grape Leaves with Zinfandel Sauce   31
Garlic Chicken Paillards   57
Green Chicken Stew with Lemon Grass, Jalapeños, and Lime   72
Lumpia   57
Petti di Pollo Ripiene (Stuffed Chicken Breasts)   155
Pollo Colorado (Chicken in Red Sauce)   144
Suprême de Volaille en Feuilletée (Chicken Breast in Puff Pastry)   24
Suprêmes de Volaille Parmesan (Boneless Chicken Breasts with Parmesan Cheese)   135

DESSERTS AND PASTRIES
Almond Semifreddo   67
Apple Crisp   115
Apple Tart "Ma Mère"   104
Brie Cheesecake   52
Caramelized Walnuts   79
Cheese Puffs   82
Chocolate Bourbon Pecan Pie   88
Chocolate Decadence   viii
Chocolate Rendezvous with Crème Anglaise and Raspberry Sauce   76
Chocolate Velvet Pie   82
Diablo Mousse Cake   110
Lime Tart   158
Macadamia Nut and Coconut Tart   69
Praline   67
Pear Tart   46
Pecan Pie   83
Pie Dough   83

Pine Nut and Apricot Tart   162
Pots de Crème au Chocolat Grand Marnier (Chocolate Custard Cream)   24
Queen of California   79
Rhubarb Pie   177
Roquefort and Apple Flan   172
Sweet Pastry Shell   104

EGGS

Huevos Rancheros (Ranch-Style Eggs)   33
Souffléed Apple Pancake   34

FISH

Cold Poached Coho Salmon with Orange Mayonnaise and Watercress Salad   73
Cold Poached Salmon with Cucumber–Sour Cream Sauce   167
Fish with Wild Mushroom-Cream Sauce   136
Four-Flavors Fish   169
Grilled Swordfish with Chili-Cumin Butter   109
Hawaiian Ono Sautéed with Butter, Lime, and Toasted Shallots   169
Medallions of Fresh Salmon with Ginger-Cilantro Sauce   76
Petrale Sole Boisliveau (Fillet of Sole Stuffed with Spinach and Endive)   112
Poached Fish with Piccata Sauce   150
Poached Salmon with Beurre Rosé and Golden Caviar   127
Red Snapper à la Bangkok   121
Salmon Fillet in a Leek Collar with Salmon Soufflé   171
Salmon with Fresh Basil Butter   98
Sautéed Sole with Hazelnut-Butter Sauce   119
Sautéed Swordfish with Tomato and Dill Sauce   27
Steamed Sole with Papaya   128

PASTA AND RISOTTO

Fettuccine with Eggplant, Black Olives, and Feta Cheese   157
Garden Lasagna   116
Grilled Summer Vegetable Pasta   66
Mushroom Risotto   142
Pasta alla Putanesca (Pasta with Piquant Tomato Sauce)   154
Pasta with Golden Caviar   142
Pumpkin Ravioli with Crème Fraîche and Chives   30
Risotto with Smoked Chicken, Artichoke, and Parmigiano   131
Risotto with Smoked Poussin, Saffron, Chanterelles, and Golden Tomatoes   71

San Remo Pasta with Roasted Tomatoes and Black Olives   86
Tomato, Basil, and Pine Nut Fettuccine   27
Wild Mushroom Lasagne   151

PIZZA

Stuffed Pizza   182

SALADS

Cabbage Salad   121
Caesar Salad   26
Chinese Chicken Salad   36
Gorgonzola-Pear Salad   49
Hunan-Style Smoked Chicken and Pasta Salad   174
Mexican Chicken Salad   36
Orange, Red Onion, and Avocado Salad with Walnut Oil Dressing   98
Spicy Turkey Salad   175
Spinach Salad with Duck Cracklings   29
Spring Chicken Salad   118
Thai Cucumber Salad   175

SANDWICHES

Chicken Salad Sandwich   55
Grilled Mozzarella and Tapenade Sandwich   54
Poached Salmon and Shallot–Cream Cheese Sandwich   139
Roasted Tomato Sandwich   54
Roast Lamb and Spinach Sandwich with Aioli and Mint Salsa   140
Smoked Chicken and Avocado Sandwich with Ginger-Sesame Mayonnaise   138

SAUCES/DRESSINGS/CHUTNEYS/CONDIMENTS

Achiote Vinaigrette   93
Aioli   140
Basil Butter   98
Béchamel Sauce   151
Beurre Blanc   19, 171
Beurre Rosé   127
Chili-Cumin Butter   109
Cilantro Sauce   148
Crème Anglaise   77
Cucumber Sour Cream Sauce   167
Fennel-Citrus Relish   51

Ginger-Cilantro Sauce   76
Ginger-Sesame Mayonnaise   138
Grape-Ginger Glaze   51
Green Chutney   39
Green Curry Paste   122
Gribiche Sauce   113
Hazelnut-Butter Sauce   119
Hunan-Style Salad Dressing   174
Joanne's Pickles   101
Lemon Vinaigrette   139
Mayonnaise   55
Mint Salsa   140
Orange Dressing   73
Orange Mayonnaise   73
Orange-Thyme Butter   50
Piccata Sauce   150
Raspberry and Rosemary Vinaigrette   51
Raspberry Sauce   77
Red Pepper Vinaigrette   50
Red Pesto   90
Salsa   33, 157
Salsa Cruda   144
Salsa Verde (Green Chili Sauce)   145
Shallot Cream Cheese   139
Spicy Toasted Sesame Sauce   100
Spinach Pesto Sauce   183
Tartar Sauce   92
Tomato Sauce   182
Vinaigrette, Mexican   37
Waghar   39
Walnut Oil Dressing   98
Walnut Oil Vinaigrette   49
Wild Mushroom-Cream Sauce   136

SOUPS

Artichoke and Leek Soup   60
Giblet Soup with Barley, Garlic, and Mushrooms   29
Green Seafood Soup   134
Roasted Tomato and Chili Soup   85
Root Vegetable Soup   115
Tom Kar Gai (Thai Chicken Soup)   164

VEGETABLES AND LEGUMES

Black Beans   33
Curried Spinach and Tomatoes   125
Eggplant with Spicy Garlic Sauce   95
Garlic Rice   57
German-Style Potato Pancakes   34
Grilled Pasilla Peppers with Salsa   157
Khaman Dhokla   39
Mandarin Green Beans, Szechwan Style   180
Roast Garlic Potatoes   26
Southwestern Corn and Cheddar "Pudding"   109
Spicy Eggplant   147
Stuffed Pasilla Chili   107

MISCELLANEOUS

"Hot" Oil   96
Caramel   172
Court Bouillon   127
Croutons   26
Fumet   73
Gremolata   29

GENERAL INDEX

Almond(s)
    and roasted garlic spread, 90
    semifreddo, 67–68
Apple(s)
    crisp, 115
    pancake, souffléed, 34
    and Roquefort flan, 172
    tart, 104
Apricot and pine nut tart, 162
Artichoke(s)
    and leek soup, 60
    in risotto with smoked chicken and
        Parmigiano, 131
Avocado
    salad with orange, red onion, and
        walnut oil dressing, 98
    and smoked chicken sandwich with
        ginger-sesame mayonnaise, 138

Bamboo shoots, 6
Barley, giblet soup with garlic, mush-
        rooms, and, 29
Basil, 11
    salmon with butter of, 98
    sweet, with chicken, 165
    tomato and pine nut fettucine with,
        27
Bay leaf, 11
Beef
    Burmese curried, 124
    dry-aged New York steak with
        Roquefort cheese sauce, 61
    green curry, 122
    with gribiche sauce, 113
    salty, 164
Beurre blanc, 171
Beurre rosé, 127

Black beans with ranch-style eggs, 33
Bourbon, chocolate pecan pie with,
        88
Bread
    Asiago cheese, 64
    cinnamon-swirl, 42–43
    Czech, 46
    fruit bran muffins, 100
    German potato, 42
    Indian fry, 162
    Italian wheat, 152
    sticky buns, 43
Butter(s), 6. See also Sauces and
        pastes
    basil, with salmon, 98
    beurre blanc, 19–20, 171
    beurre rosé, 127
    chili-cumin, with grilled swordfish,
        109
    clarified, 8
    composed, 20
    hazelnut, 119
    orange-thyme, 50

Cabbage salad with barbecued
        chicken, 121
Cake(s)
    almond semifreddo, 67–68
    Brie cheesecake, 52
    Chocolate Decadence, vi
    Diablo Mousse, 110
    Queen of California, 79
California cuisine, 4–5
    ingredients used in, 6–16
    techniques of, 17–19
Caraway, Czech bread, 46
Caviar
    golden, and beurre rosé with

salmon, 127
    golden, with pasta, 142
Cheese
    Asiago bread, 64
    Brie cheesecake, 52
    cojita, with ancho chili marinade,
        sweet peppers, and cold roasted
        eggplant, 160
    corn and pudding of cheddar, 109
    creamed feta with roasted peppers,
        45
    Emmenthaler, 45
    feta, with eggplant, olives, and fet-
        tuccine, 157
    grilled mozzarella, and tapenade
        sandwich, 54
    herbed cream, 64
    Parmesan, 15
    Parmesan, with boneless chicken
        breasts, 135
    Parmigiano-Reggiano, in risotto
        with smoked chicken and arti-
        choke, 131
    pear salad with Gorgonzola, 49
    puffs, 82
    Roquefort, and apple flan, 172
    sauce of Roquefort, with New York
        steak, 61
    shallot-cream, and salmon sand-
        wich, 139
Chefs, development of, 4
Chicken
    barbequed, with cabbage salad, 121
    Hunan-style smoked, and pasta
        salad, 174
    liver mousse pâté, 88
    in red sauce, 144
    smoked, and avocado sandwich

Chicken (*continued*)
with ginger-sesame mayonnaise, 138
smoked, with artichokes, rice, and Parmigiano, 131
with sweet basil, 165
Chicken breast(s), 6
bon bon chicken, 96
boneless, with Parmesan cheese, 135
Chinese salad, 36
curry, 165
garlic paillards, 57–58
lumpia, 57–58
Mexican salad, 37
minced appetizer, 179
in puff pastry, 24
risotto with saffron, chanterelles, golden tomatoes, and smoked, 71
salad, 118
salad, sandwich of, 55
stew with lemon grass, jalapeños, and lime, 72
stuffed, 155
Thai chicken soup, 164
Chilies, 6–8. *See also* Peppers
butter of cumin and, with grilled swordfish, 109
chicken in red sauce, 144
dried, 8
fresh, 7
Fresno, 7
green chutney, 39
jalapeño, 7
jalapeños, lemon grass, and lime with green chicken stew, 72
marinade of ancho, with sweet peppers, cojita cheese, and cold roasted eggplant, 160
pasilla, poblano, and Anaheim, 7–8
in roast lamb and spinach sandwich with aioli and mint salsa, 140

salsa with ranch-style eggs, 33
sauce of green, 145
serrano, 7
serrano, in green curry paste, 122
soup of roasted tomato and, 85
stuffed pasilla, 107
Thai, 7
Chives, pumpkin ravioli with crème fraîche and, 30
Chocolate
bourbon pecan pie, 88
Chocolate Decadence cake, vi
custard cream, 24
Diablo Mousse cake, 110
glaze, 79
pâté with crème anglaise and raspberry sauce, 76–77
Queen of California cake, 79–80
velvet pie, 82–83
Chutney, green, 39
Cilantro, 11–12
garnish, 39
ginger, sauce with salmon, 76
sauce with seafood-stuffed summer squash, 148
Cinnamon
sticky buns, 43
swirl loaves, 42–43
Coconut
garnish, 39
and macadamia nut tart, 69
milk, 8–9
milk, in green curry beef, 122
Cooking in restaurants, 2–3
Corn
cheddar pudding and, 109
timbale with red pepper vinaigrette, 49–50
Court bouillon, 127
Cranberry beans in braised lamb shanks with shellbeans, tomato, and herbs, 130
Crème anglaise, 77

Crème fraîche, 9
pumpkin ravioli with chives and, 30
Crème pâtissière, 104
Croutons, in Caesar salad, 26
Cucumber(s)
Joanne's pickles, 101
salad of Thai, 175
and sour cream sauce with cold poached salmon, 167
Cumin, butter of chili and, with grilled swordfish, 109
Custard
chocolate, with Grand Marnier, 24
Roquefort and apple flan, 172

David, Narsai, vi
Dill, swordfish with sauce of tomato and, 27
Duck
cracklings of, with spinach salad, 29–30
liver mousse, 147
sausage wrapped in grape leaves with Zinfandel sauce, 31

Eggplant(s)
black olives, feta cheese, and fettucine with, 157
cake with tomato jelly, 103
cold roasted, with ancho chili marinade, sweet peppers, and cojita cheese, 160
in grilled summer vegetable pasta, 66
spicy, 147–48
with spicy garlic sauce, 95
Eggs, ranch-style, 33
Endive, sole stuffed with spinach and, 112

Fennel-citrus relish, 51
Fish. *See also* Salmon; Sole; Swordfish
   buying and storing, 17
   four-flavors rockfish, 169
   four sauces for grilled, 50–51
   green seafood soup, 134
   Hawaiian ono, 169
   poached, with piccata sauce, 150
   red snapper à la Bangkok, 121–22
   sauce, 9–10
   seafood-stuffed summer squash with cilantro sauce, 148
   tuna and salmon appetizer, 62
   with wild mushroom-cream sauce, 136

Galangal, 10
   in Thai chicken soup, 164
Garlic, 10
   almond spread with roasted, 90
   chicken paillards, 57–58
   giblet soup with barley, mushrooms, and, 29
   peeling and using, 17–18
   potatoes roasted with, 26
   rice, 57
   spicy sauce with eggplant, 95
Giblet soup with barley, garlic, and mushrooms, 29
Ginger, 11
   cilantro sauce with salmon, 76
   grape, glaze, 51
   sesame mayonnaise with chicken and avocado sandwich, 138
Glaze
   chocolate, 79
   grape-ginger, 51
Grand Marnier
   chocolate custard cream with, 24
   in crème anglaise for chocolate pâté with raspberry sauce, 76–77
Grapefruit, fennel-citrus relish, 51

Grape-ginger glaze, 51
Grape leaves, duck sausage wrapped in, with Zinfandel sauce, 31
Green beans, Mandarin, Szechwan-style, 180
Gremolata, 29
Grilling foods, 18–19

Hawaiian ono, 169
Hazelnuts, sole with butter of, 119
Herbs, 11–12
   basil, 11
   bay leaf, 11
   braised lamb shanks with shellbeans, tomato, and, 130
   cilantro, 11–12
   oregano and marjoram, 12
   tarragon, 12
   thyme, 12
Hoisin sauce with lamb, 74

Lamb
   braised shanks with shellbeans, tomato, and herbs, 130
   marinated grilled leg of, 106
   rack of, Assyrian, vi–vii
   sandwich of spinach and, with aioli and mint salsa, 140
   sautéed marinated, with Thai peppers, red onion, and hoisin sauce, 74
Leek(s)
   achiote vinaigrette appetizer in a terrine, 93
   and artichoke soup, 60
   with salmon, 171
Lemon(s)
   dried leaves of, 9
   fennel-citrus relish, 51
   vinaigrette in poached salmon and shallot-cream cheese sandwich, 139

Lemon grass, 12–13
   chicken stew with jalapeños, lime, and, 72
   sauce of, for lumpia, 58
Lime(s)
   and butter with toasted shallots and Hawaiian ono, 169
   dried, and dried leaves of, 9
   green chicken stew with lemon grass, jalapeños, and, 72
   and lime leaves, dried, 9
   tart, 158

Macadamia nut and coconut tart, 69
Makrud/macrut (dried lime), 9
Marinade
   ancho chili, 160
   garlic chicken paillards, 57
   green chicken stew, 72
   grilled lamb, 106
   rack of lamb, vi–vii
Marjoram, 12
Mesquite wood for grilling, 18
Mint salsa, 140
Muffins, fruit bran, 100
Mushrooms, 13–14
   cèpe, 14
   chanterelle, 13
   chanterelle, in risotto with smoked poussin, saffron, and golden tomatoes, 71
   cultivated, 13
   dried, 14
   field, 13
   fish with sauce of cream and wild, 136
   giblet soup with barley, garlic, and, 29
   morel, 13
   and pecan pate, 133
   risotto, 142
   wild, 13
   wild, in lasagna, 151

Olive oil, 14–15
  in aioli, 140
Olives
  eggplant, feta cheese, and fettuccine
    with black, 157
  roasted tomatoes with San Remo
    pasta and black, 86
  tapenade and grilled mozzarella
    sandwich, 54
Onion(s)
  pancakes, 40
  red, and orange and avocado salad
    with walnut oil dressing, 98
  red, with lamb, Thai peppers, and
    hoisin sauce, 74
Ono, Hawaiian, 169
Orange(s)
  fennel-citrus relish, 51
  salad of red onion, avocado, and,
    98
  salmon with salad and dressing of,
    73
  thyme butter sauce, 50
Oregano, 12

Pancakes
  German-style potato, 34
  onion uthapa, 40
  souffléed apple, 34
Papaya with sole, 128
Parmesan cheese, 15
Pasta
  fettuccine with eggplant, black ol-
    ives, and feta cheese, 157
  fettuccine with tomatoes, basil, and
    pine nuts, 27
  garden lasagna, 116
  with golden caviar, 142
  grilled summer vegetable, 66
  with piquant tomato sauce, 154
  pumpkin ravioli with crème fraîche
    and chives, 30
  roasted tomatoes and black olives
    with, 86

salad and Hunan-style smoked
    chicken, 174
  wild mushroom lasagna, 151
Pastry. See also Cake(s); Pie(s); Tart(s)
  apple crisp, 115
  cheese puffs, 82
  chicken breast in puff, 24
Pear(s)
  salad of Gorgonzola cheese and, 49
  tart, 46–47
Pecan(s)
  apple crisp, 115
  chocolate bourbon pie with, 88
  and mushroom pâté, 133
  pie, 83
Peppers. See also Chilies
  bell, 7
  bell, in red pesto, 90
  grilled pasilla, with salsa, 157
  in grilled summer vegetable pasta,
    66
  roasted, with creamed feta, 45
  roasting and peeling, 19
  sweet, with ancho chili marinade,
    cojita cheese, and cold roasted
    eggplant, 160
  Thai, with lamb, red onion, and
    hoisin sauce, 74
  vinaigrette of red, with corn tim-
    bale, 49–50
Pesto
  red, 90
  spinach, 183
Pickles, Joanne's, 101
Pie(s)
  chocolate, 82
  chocolate bourbon pecan, 88
  pecan, 83
  rhubarb, 177
Pine nut(s)
  and apricot tart, 162
  tomato, basil, and fettuccine with,
    27
Pizza, stuffed, 182

Potato(es)
  bread, German, 42
  in green seafood soup, 134
  pancakes, German-style, 34
  roast garlic, 27
  root vegetable soup, 115
Poussin, risotto, saffron, chanterelles,
    and golden tomatoes with, 71
Pumpkin ravioli with creme fraiche
    and chives, 30

Raspberry
  and rosemary vinaigrette, 51
  sauce with chocolate pâté and
    crème anglaise, 76–77
Recipes, development of, 2–3
Red snapper à la Bangkok, 121–22
Rhubarb pie, 177
Rice
  garlic, 57
  mushroom risotto, 142
  risotto with smoked chicken, arti-
    choke, and Parmigiano, 131
  risotto with smoked poussin, saf-
    fron, chanterelles, and golden
    tomatoes, 71
  Thai perfumed, 16
Rockfish, four-flavors fish, 169
Rosemary and raspberry vinaigrette,
    51

Saffron, risotto with smoked poussin,
    chanterelles, golden tomatoes
    and, 71
Salad
  cabbage with barbecued chicken,
    121
  Caesar, 26
  chicken, sandwich, 55
  Chinese chicken, 36
  cold poached coho salmon with or-
    ange mayonnaise and watercress,
    73

Gorgonzola-pear, 49

Mexican chicken, 37

orange, red onion, and avocado, with walnut oil dressing, 98

pasta, with smoked chicken, 174

spicy turkey, 175

spinach, with duck cracklings, 29–30

spring chicken, 118

Thai cucumber, 175

watercress, cold poached coho salmon with orange mayonnaise and, 73

Salad dressing

achiote vinaigrette, 93

aioli, 140

axonometric appetizer, 62

chicken and pasta salad, 174

ginger-sesame mayonnaise, 138

lemon vinaigrette, 139

orange, for watercress salad, 73

orange mayonnaise for salmon, 73

raspberry and rosemary vinaigrette, 51

red pepper vinaigrette, 50

spicy turkey, 175

vinaigrette, 37

walnut oil, 98

walnut oil vinaigrette, 49

Salmon

appetizer with tuna, 62

with basil butter, 98

cold poached, with cucumber-sour cream sauce, 167

cold poached coho, with orange mayonnaise and watercress salad, 73

fillet of, in leek collar with salmon soufflé, 171

with ginger-cilantro sauce, 76

poached, with beurre rosé and golden caviar, 127

shallot-cream cheese sandwich with poached, 139

Sauces and pastes. *See also* Butter(s)

bechamel, 151

for chicken and Parmesan cheese, 135

cilantro, 148

crème anglaise, 77

crème fraîche, 30

crème pâtissière, 104

cucumber-sour cream, 167

fish, 9–10

ginger-cilantro, with salmon, 76

green curry, 122

gribiche, 113

for grilled fish, 50–51

hoisin, with lamb, 74

lumpia, 58

mint salsa, 140

for mushroom and pecan pate, 133

piccata, 150

raspberry, 76

red pesto, 90

Roquefort, 61

salsa cruda, 144

salsa verde, 145

salsa with pasilla peppers, 157

salsa with ranch-style eggs, 33

sesame, 100

spicy garlic, 95

spicy sesame, 100

spinach pesto, 183

for stuffed sole, 112

tartar, 92

tomato, 154, 182

tomato and dill, with swordfish, 27

wild mushroom, 136

Zinfandel, 31

Sesame seeds, spicy toasted sauce of, 100

Shallot(s)

and cream cheese sandwich with poached salmon, 139

toasted, with lime and Hawaiian ono, 169

Sole

fillet of, with spinach and endive, 112

with hazelnut-butter sauce, 119

steamed, with papaya, 128

Soup

artichoke and leek, 60

Burmese curried beef stew, 124

giblet, with barley, garlic, and mushrooms, 29

green chicken stew, 72

green seafood, 134

roasted tomato and chili, 85

root vegetable, 115

Thai chicken Tom Kar Gai, 164

venison picadillo, 161

Sour cream, sauce of cucumber and, with cold poached salmon, 167

Spinach

curried, and tomatoes, 125

in green seafood soup, 134

pesto sauce, 183

and roast lamb sandwich with aioli and mint salsa, 140

salad with duck cracklings, 29–30

sole stuffed with endive and, 112

Split peas, cornbread of yellow, 39

Squash

in garden lasagna, 116

seafood-stuffed, with cilantro sauce, 148

Stocks, 20–21

Strawberries in fruit bran muffins, 100

Swordfish

grilled, with chili-cumin butter, 109

with tomato and dill sauce, 27

Tamarind, 16

Tapenade, 54

Tarragon, 12, 92

Tart(s)

apple, 104

Tart(s) (continued)
  lime, 158
  macadamia nut and coconut, 69
  pear, 46–47
  pine nut and apricot, 162
Thyme, 12
  orange, butter sauce, 50
Tomato(es)
  basil and pine nut fettuccine with, 27
  black olives with pasta and roasted, 86
  curried spinach and, 125
  golden, in risotto with smoked poussin, saffron, and chante-relles, 71
  jelly with eggplant cake, 103
  piquant, sauce with pasta, 154
  Roma, in red pesto, 90
  salsa with ranch-style eggs, 33

sandwich of roasted, 54
shellbeans, herbs, and braised lamb shanks with, 130
soup of chili and roasted, 85
sun-dried, 15
swordfish with sauce of dill and, 27
Tuna appetizer with salmon, 62
Turkey, spicy salad with, 175
Turnips, root vegetable soup, 115

Venison picadillo stew, 161
Vinegar
  achiote vinaigrette appetizer with leek terrine, 93
  in piccata sauce with poached fish, 150
  raspberry and rosemary vinaigrette, 51

red pepper vinaigrette with fresh corn timbale, 49–50
tartar sauce, 92
vinaigrette salad dressing, 37

Waghar, 39
Walnut(s)
  apple crisp, 115
  caramelized, with Queen of Califor-nia cake, 79–80
  oil dressing with orange, red onion, and avocado salad, 98
Watercress, coho salmon with orange mayonnaise and salad of, 73
Wine, cooking, 16
Wonton skins appetizer, 62

Zinfandel sauce, 30